CATHOLIC
PRAYER

CATHOLIC PRAYER

Pray-er + Words + Gestures +
Reading + Jesus + Eucharist +
Models + Politics + Stages

Lawrence S. Cunningham

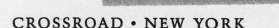

CROSSROAD · NEW YORK

1989

The Crossroad Publishing Company
370 Lexington Avenue, New York, N.Y. 10017

Printed in the United States of America

Library of Congress Cataloging-in-Publication Data

Cunningham, Lawrence.
    Catholic prayer : pray-er, words, gestures, reading, Jesus,
Eucharist, models, stages, politics / Lawrence S. Cunningham.
        p.   cm.
    Includes index.
    Bibliography: p.
    ISBN 0–8245–0930–7
    1. Spirituality—Catholic Church. 2. Prayer. 3. Catholic Church—
Doctrines. 4. Catholic Church—Liturgy.   I. Title.
BX2350.65.C86   1989
248.3'2—dc19   88–36462
                                                                    CIP

CONTENTS

Introduction   1

Chapter One | PRAY-ER   7

Chapter Two | WORDS   28

Chapter Three | GESTURES   49

Chapter Four | READING   69

Chapter Five | JESUS   90

Chapter Six | EUCHARIST   111

Chapter Seven | MODELS   131

Chapter Eight | POLITICS   151

Chapter Nine | STAGES   172

Appendix: Teaching about Prayer   193

Index   201

INTRODUCTION

For the past decade I have been thinking about the nature of the Catholic tradition to discover and elucidate what it means to be a Catholic (by which, following the common usage, I mean a Roman Catholic) as opposed, say, to be a Protestant. My suspicion has been that to be a Catholic, at least when one is Catholic by choice, is to assume a certain style of life and to embrace the values of a certain tradition and worldview. My self-imposed subject, then, was to sort out the nature of that style and the broad parameters of the Catholic tradition and worldview. In this quest I have tried to stay away from any visionary approach to Catholicism and close to the tradition of Catholicism as it is palpable, at least from the peculiar angle of my own experiences, which are North American and academic and middle class. My focus has been further narrowed by my methodological exclusion of those other Christian bodies who rightly proclaim their belief in the "One, Holy, *Catholic*, and Apostolic Church." I trust that readers will understand that the exclusion is methodological and not ideological.

Some of the fruits of my thinking have been published in books like *The Catholic Heritage* (1983), *The Catholic Experience* (1985), and *The Catholic Faith: An Introduction* (1987). It would be rash to think of those books as "scholarly," for they were intended not for the academy but for the putative thinking person in the pew (or on the porch of the church) who might be as fascinated by Catholicism as I have been.

1

Launching those books has been, at best, a kind of signal to my fellow Catholics that the subject is worth thinking about; that there are ways to think about the church; and, finally, when one cuts back into the heart of the matter, there is Jesus the Christ who is at the center and heart of all that we are about or should be about. In that sense, at least, my approach has been both phenomenological and theological. My desire is to discover an irenic way of talking about the communalities of Catholicism at a time when the church is sorely divided into factions of both the Right and the Left. We know what separates these camps. What, broadly considered, holds them together?

When one thinks about an enormous topic like the Catholic tradition there are more directions and byways to follow than one can handle within manageable bounds. This book is proof of that. The history of Christianity is filled with classic works on prayer beginning with treatises of the second century and coming down to the present day. Never once was I tempted to add to the body of that literature nor even to trace its main shape. My object has been a good deal more modest: to think about prayer in the context of the tradition that has occupied my attention over these past years.

This, then, is not a handbook or manual on how to pray. Such volumes fill many bookshelves with more coming from the presses each year. It is a book that attempts to reflect on the place of prayer in the Catholic tradition. I think that each religious tradition has its own "flavor," and in no way am I arguing that Catholics pray better or more authentically than others. My attention to the Catholic tradition comes in obedience to the dictum that one should focus only on those things that one knows something about.

Nor is this book a systematic historical or theological treatise on prayer in the Catholic tradition. The work is systematic only in the sense that it begins with the things I have known at first hand as a Catholic (e.g., going to Mass; teaching my kids to say grace before meals, and so on) and things I have read about in the rather promiscuous way I read things. Aristotle says that people, by nature, desire to know and, being a person, I wanted to know a bit about how prayer "fits" into the Catholic picture. This book, then, is a product of my simple desire to understand things a bit better. That an argument does not evolve systematically from chapter to chapter can be explained by the fact that certain ideas kept coming around in various forms and because I wanted this book to have at least the air of a meditative and ruminative consideration of the subject.

I write from within the Catholic faith community. This work does not count as foundational theology; it assumes the foundations and builds upon them. In a sense, the kind of theology—if it is theology—that seems most useful for my ends is that older tradition of theology—monastic theology, if you will—that accepts as a given the Bible, the tradition of thinkers and mystics in the church, the liturgical sources, the conciliar decrees, etc., and attempts to make some sense of them from the particular (and very limited!) location where, existentially and culturally, I find myself: as an American middle-aged Catholic lurching toward the end of the second millennium of the Christian Era. This is not to say that I am ignorant of, or indifferent to, the work of historians, exegetes, or critics. It is to say that I am a consumer of, rather than a contributor to, those enterprises.

To focus on prayer seems crucial because, in the last analysis, prayer is at the heart of religious belief in general and the Catholic tradition in particular. As I worked through the topics that make up the chapters of this book I also spent a good deal of time reading prayers. It strikes me—hardly an original insight—that the body of prayers which have come down to us both from liturgical sources and from the devotional tradition are an inestimable theological resource. Thus, to underscore that fact, I have appended a prayer to the conclusion of each chapter together with a brief excursus on that prayer. Those prayers and the brief commentaries are meant only to emphasize my conviction, already stated, that such prayers in the tradition merit some close attention.

My focus on the topic of prayer derives not from any personal advanced experiential knowledge of the topic. My interest in the whole subject springs from the deep conviction that theology ought to be a holistic enterprise which, while seeking that understanding of faith which Anselm of Canterbury recommends, will include not only the doctrines of the faith but their expression in the devotional, liturgical, and mystical life of the church. My model, to the extent that I have followed a model, is the stream of reflective theology in the Catholic tradition that is called *Sacra Pagina*—a theology that turns to the scriptures in order to meditate on its truth(s) and, from that meditation, to turn to the contemplation of the essential mystery which stands at the heart of human reality: God. I realize that such a strategy may seem to beg the question in a fideistic fashion by not answering the prior question: Can we pray at all? My only response to such an objection is that people, in fact, pray, and prayers are a part of this tradition. What this all means is of interest to me. To that degree I would see myself as working broadly in the phenomenological tradition of inquiry.

Another motif that runs through this book is the conviction that prayer can be understood not only as a discrete activity but as a relationship that is embedded in the very act of being a believer: In a real sense, to believe and to pray are interchangeable terms if only because the believer, in some fashion or other, must name the object of belief. Readers, I trust, will forgive the neologism *pray-er*, but it is a curious fact about English that there is no single word to express "the person who prays" except *worshiper*, which carries with it certain liturgical or formal resonances that did not satisfy my theological needs. Nor did the term *supplicant* or the other words that I entertained as possibilities seem right. By the term *pray-er* I am creating a neologism that strains to express the Latin word *orans*, literally "praying," referring to the person who prays. Readers may feel reassured that it is the only neologism that I have created in the book—not a bad record for a theologian today.

A good deal of attention in the book will be devoted to the liturgy because the liturgy is Christian prayer *par excellence* as well as an essential sign of being a Catholic. Because I am concerned with prayer as relationship and prayer as an identifiable reality (as a literature and as an activity both official and unofficial), this book will have at least one crosscurrent in it as it attempts to say something somewhat novel (prayer exists before prayers are said) while, at the same time, discussing something very traditional: that the accumulated prayers of the church are a basic source of theology and belief. *Lex orandi, lex credendi.*

In my discussion of prayer I did not consider mysticism by that name, but the validity of mysticism is assumed and is treated, in various places, as simple prayer. This was a judgment call on my part based on my conviction that the term *mysticism* carries with it a kind of baggage which I had neither the time nor space to carry in a book this short. Simple prayer (or contemplative prayer) is available to all believers and most likely is frequently experienced by large numbers of people without being named as such.

A word about procedures:

For reasons of tidiness and pedagogy I have omitted footnotes from this book. At the end of each chapter is a list of books either referred to in the text or of use to those who wish to follow topics in more depth. Some of the ideas in the book were expressed in other forms in essays that I have contributed to various journals and magazines, but everything was rewritten for this book. Some of those articles and essays are mentioned in the appropriate reading lists in various chapters throughout the book. Chapter 3 of this work will appear in abbreviated form in *Studies in Formative Spirituality* (May 1989).

Most of my adult life has been spent in the classroom and my instincts are almost always pedagogical ones. This is by no means a textbook, but I would wish that some might find it useful in the classroom setting. To foster that possibility the book has, as a kind of coda, a very brief excursus on teaching about prayer. My purpose, in providing these bare pedagogical strategies, is to encourage others to think about the prayer tradition of Christianity. My suggestions are meant for the individual who wishes to pursue them or for the teacher who might wish others to use them as academic exercises. One could do worse things with one's time than try the contemplative exercise of composing prayers.

Finally, I have the happy task of putting in print a few words of thanks to various people. This book was begun while I was still on the religion faculty of the Florida State University; to my colleagues there, and especially Walter L. Moore, Jr., who chairs the department, I owe many thanks. I finished the draft after I had joined the theology department of the University of Notre Dame. A special word of gratitude is due Father Richard McBrien who chairs the department in such a way that there is time to think and write. Many good books on prayer have come my way thanks to Brother Patrick Hart of the Abbey of Gethsemani. Frank Oveis, among editors *facile princeps*, has been a good friend and stern critic. Margaret Steinfels, now editor of *Commonweal*, sent me a fat box of books to review for the journal *Church*; those books and the exercise of reviewing them were a rich experience for me as I was working on this book.

This book, as always, is for Cecilia, Sarah Mary, and Julia Clare.

1

PRAY-ER

I waited patiently for the Lord;
He inclined to me and heard my prayer.

Psalm 40:1

The late Mircea Eliade was a profoundly original student of religion. His contributions to the various aspects of religious behavior, from myth and ritual to the character of religious time and the sacralization of space, have had an immense impact on the field of religion. What is most fundamental in Eliade's phenomenological approach to the study of religion, however, is his basic conviction that religion is not adherence to a creed but a mode of being in the world. In his highly regarded book *The Sacred and the Profane* Eliade begins with the observation that what separates the religious person (*homo religiosus*) from the profane person is the former's experience of the Sacred as it breaks into his or her world. Let us underscore that this is not merely a conviction but an experience. The religious person is one who senses the Sacred as a dimension of the human enterprise.

When one translates Eliade's insight into the concrete particularities of biblical religion, it means, simply, that the God of Abraham, Isaac, and Jacob (as well as the God of Jesus) is not an idea or an ideal but a person who is encountered. That fact leaps out at us when we read the Bible at even the most superficial level. An example makes the point clearly. Consider this passage which initiates the narrative of salvation history:

Now the Lord said to Abram, "Go from your country and your kindred and your father's house to the land that I will show you. And I will make of you a great nation, and I will bless you, and make your name great so that you will be a blessing. I will bless those who bless you and him who curses you will I curse; and by you all the families of the earth shall bless themselves." So Abram went, as the Lord told him. (Gen. 12:1–4)

There are a number of things to be noted about that short selection. First, God speaks without establishing any credentials. God simply says "Go." Secondly, there is no corresponding inquiry from Abram (e.g., Why should I go?); verse four puts it tersely: "So Abram went." Finally, one must note some things "behind" the text: the assumption is that we are dealing with a conversation between two persons (Did Abram see God? Did he literally hear God? Was he startled? Frightened? Dubious?) in which there is a link of understanding. God speaks; Abram reacts. That dynamic also intimates that there is one who orders and one who obeys. To put it another way: there is superior and inferior. Above all, however, is the bare fact of relationship.

It is also clear from that text that the central issue of the story is the interchange between God and Abram. There is very little background to the story; it is a dialogue with the narrative line supplying the necessary reaction on the part of Abram to the communication of God. Abram hears and, in that hearing, acts. As Erich Auerbach, in a famous formulation about biblical narrative, puts it: Everything in the Bible is in the foreground.

Behind and prior to all the things we can say about that text there is Eliade's insight: What makes Abram a *homo religiosus* is his existential acceptance of the fact that God can, in fact, speak to him. Prior to what is said there is the fact of the saying. Precisely because Abram lives as a person who responds to the Other we call him a person of faith.

My conviction is that every encounter between a person and God in the Bible could be analyzed in roughly the same fashion. Those encounters are characterized by the intrusion of the Sacred and the response of the person. The nature of this interchange may differ but the bare fact of the encounter is clear. If one wanted to phrase the matter in somewhat different terms it would be that there is always another pole against which the characters of the Bible must be seen if there is to be any clear sense of who they are or what they are about. This may happen by way of response (Abram) or resistance (Jonah) or puzzlement (Samuel). Whatever the response, the poles remain. The negation of the relationship, just to turn the examples around, demands either the beginning of the relationship by conversion (e.g., Saints Peter and Thomas in their denial) or the turning into the self in a way that breaks the relationship with the divine as the *non serviam* of the rebellious angels or in the case of Judas. Biblical people either are or are not in some kind of relationship; that relationship is one of faith rooted in a sense of dialogue.

What has this to do with prayer? Fundamentally, what we wish to argue in this book is that the action we call prayer is, prior to its formulation into words, songs, gestures, etc., that basic relation between God and the person who encounters God. To say it somewhat differently: The person of faith is the person of prayer and vice versa; faith and prayer are, if not interchangeable terms, two sides of a common coin. If there is a basic thesis to this chapter (and this book as a whole) it is this: that prayer is, primarily and fundamentally, a way of being before it is saying, doing, or gesturing. To be a believer is to be a pray-er. What separates religious belief from, say, a philosophy of life is the presence of prayer and the capacity to pray.

That formulation of the matter might seem a bit eccentric since we tend to think of prayer (the English word, via the Romance languages, comes from the Latin *precare*, to beseech or to petition) from our perspective of speaking to God. If, however, we go back a step and consider prayer, first and foremost, as relationship, the point we are attempting to make becomes less exotic. When we fully understand the nature of this relationship that is prayer we will then be in a better position to see how that relationship becomes formulated in words, gestures, and rituals both in the lives of individuals and in communities. Our first task, then, is to revise the notion of prayer away from the idea of discrete acts to an idea of fundamental relationship.

Without anticipating the fuller argument of the next chapter we can note, at this point, that our plan is to argue for the idea of prayer as relationship in the first instance and subsequently to make the case that such relationships are always articulated in words and/or gestures. The link, then, between the one who prays (the pray-er) and the prayers he or she utters is an intimate one. Indeed, to appreciate fully that nexus keeps us from considering prayer in terms of formulae.

The notion of prayer as relationship is not an insight peculiar to this book. While it is true (alas!) that prayer receives very little systematic treatment from theologians as they develop the traditional concerns of systematics, the centrality of prayer as relationship has been not only a commonplace in the tradition of monastic and aescetical theology but also a central concern of those who have attempted, either through phenomenological or psychological analysis, to understand what is essential to the religious mode of being. To specify that point a bit let us consider two classic works on the life of the spirit written in this century.

When William James came to the conclusion of his Gifford Lectures, which were to become the now classic *The Varieties of Religious Experience* (1902), he turned his attention to the essence of religion. In lecture twenty James summed up the meaning of the religious life by setting out three general observations:

1. that the visible world is part of a more spiritual universe from which it draws its chief significance;

2. that union or harmonious relation with that higher universe is our true end;

3. that prayer or inner communion with the spirit thereof—be that spirit "God" or "Law"—is a process wherein work is really done, and spiritual energy flows in and produces effects, either psychological or material, within the phenomenal world.

The centrality of prayer as the link between the believer and the "spiritual universe" of which James speaks had already been spelled out by James in the previous lecture. Speaking of the characteristics of the religious life, James examines, in a rather cursory manner, aesthetics, sacrifice, and confession; he then turns to the issue of prayer which he says demands a longer consideration. He asserts his conviction that prayer is the very center of religion. He quotes with evident approbation the sentiments of the liberal Protestant theologian Auguste Sabatier who argued that prayer conceived of in the widest possible way as communion can be considered the very soul and essence of religion. Sabatier noted that prayer was the one sure thing that a philosopher could point to in order to distinguish the religious sensibility from that of the aesthetic moment or moral sentiment. James then concludes that prayer as "something that is transacting" is found at every stage of religious life and is its most characteristic feature. The word "transacting," of course, means that there is a link or a dialogue going on.

It is the simple observation of Sabatier that prayer is the one sure thing which separates philosophy from religion that forms the heart of this present work. Prayer is not a by-product of religion; it is its defining characteristic.

A generation after James delivered his famous lectures the German scholar and pioneer ecumenist Friedrich Heiler published his now classic study *Das Gebet* (1918; English translation under the title *Prayer* in 1932). Heiler's book was a comprehensive attempt at describing prayer in the world's religions from the preliterate to the historical religions of both East and West. Later in this book we will make use of (without agreeing with) some of Heiler's observations. At this point we merely want to underscore his basic starting point, which agrees with James's thesis that prayer is a fundamental characteristic of all religion. In the introductory sections of his book, Heiler argues that prayer is the central phenomenon of religion. Under the various forms of prayer (rites, sacraments, words, etc.) there is the irreducible connectedness with the Divine. Heiler was convinced that one could read back through the forms of prayer in such a way as to uncover the very foundation stones of religion itself. Interestingly enough, he cites with approval the same Auguste Sabatier whom James had used with such admiration.

What one finds in both James and Heiler is the conviction that prayer is central to the religious enterprise. Indeed, the forms of prayer are articulations of the deepest meaning and the most dynamic forces working in religious faith. Prayer, understood at that level, is relationship. There is prayer, and then it receives form as "prayer(s)" as we normally understand the term. But first there is the relationship.

The relationship of which we speak, we must insist, is not one between equals. Eliade, drawing heavily from the classic study by Rudolph Otto, *The Idea of the Holy*, insists that the breakthrough of the Sacred (Eliade uses *Sacred* rather than *God* because he studies religion from a universalistic stance) is always of a special and peculiar kind; it is, to use Otto's phrase, "totally other" (*Ganz Andere*). God is God and not some vague thing-out-there or sentiment-in-here which we grasp as slightly larger than ourselves. Nor is it the conclusion we come to because of some analysis or through some inductive process. God is that Other, to use Martin Buber's lovely phrase, who can never be expressed but only addressed.

That relationship receives its peak expression in those showings-forth of God (technically called *theophanies*) in which humans sense their radical differentness from God. When Moses confronted the presence of God in the burning bush he "hid his face, for he was afraid of God" (Exod. 3:6) and, on the mountaintop when he received the Law, God was like a "devouring fire" (Exod. 24:16). What Moses experienced in his day was not dissimilar to the experiences of the apostles who climbed the mount of Transfiguration or Saul on the road to Damascus or the visionary experiences of John on Patmos.

Not all of the revelations of God are as baroque as those mentioned above. The presence of God can be subtle. There is a difference between the voice of God in the whirlwind experienced by Job (see Job 38:1ff.) and the quietly persistent call of God to the young Samuel (1 Sam. 3:4ff.), just as there is a difference between the theophanies of the New Testament and the quiet recognition of the Lord when the apostles ate with the "stranger" on the road to Emmaus.

Whether the revelations of the Divine are theatrical or simple the bond is there between the One who reveals and the one who receives and assents to that revelation. In that reception a person comes to a new kind of experiential knowledge which is quite new and quite unique. That experiential knowledge is, simultaneously, faith and prayer. The whole dynamic of biblical religion is rooted in the conviction that humans do not have to search for God; biblical religion is not an ascesis of knowledge by which we learn how to ascend to God. Biblical religion founds itself on the conviction that God first speaks to us with the expectation that we, in turn, can speak back to God. Saint Paul frames that insight with both elegance and economy: "When the time had fully come, God sent his son, born of a woman, born under the law, to redeem those who were under the law, so that we might receive adoption as sons. And because you are sons, God has sent the Spirit of his Son into our hearts, crying, 'Abba! Father' " (Gal. 4:4–6).

After his death on August 19, 1662, those who prepared the body of Blaise Pascal for burial found, sewn into his coat, a paper which later generations would come to call Pascal's Memorial. Dated November 23, 1654, it recounts a profound religious experience that Pascal had between "half-past ten in the evening until half-past midnight." In the center of the page Pascal wrote the word "Fire" and, under that, the sentence fragment: "God of Abraham, God of Isaac, God of Jacob, not of philosophers and scholars." There then follows a whole series of sentence fragments and single phrases that expressed certitude and joy as well as invocations of the name of Jesus and sentiments of conversion and repentance. The tattered memorial, with its repeated foldings and creases, was carried by Pascal at all times as a reminder of this deeply personal encounter with God.

The most startling phrase in the memorial is the one that contrasts the God of the biblical patriarchs and the god of the philosophers. For Pascal, the night of November 23 was an encounter with the Totally Other and not merely the intuition of a trained mathematician and philosopher, even though he was both. The God whom Pascal encountered was not simply an object out there to be seen or marveled at (contemplated?) but an Other who deeply touched him in a manner that he felt obliged to memorialize. The god of the philosophers can be described as an intellectual conclusion, but the God of the patriarchs can be named with the expectation of response. That latter naming carries with it the essential notion of answer.

Pascal's experience is hardly unique in the annals of spirituality. I cite it not because his experience is normative but because those moments in which God is experientially known help us grasp the seriousness of the relationship that exists inchoately in all true relational prayer. In that sense the witness of the mystics and spiritual masters/mistresses is invaluable. They highlight, as it were, the nexus between the pray-er and God. They write in bold strokes what most of us experience, as it were, at the threshold.

Curiously enough, our century, often decried for its godlessness and its secularity, has given witness to this relational prayer in great abundance. More curiously, this phenomenon is observable in some great souls who have been profound pray-ers but who have not been able to articulate an orthodox credo subsequent to their life of prayer. In them we find a naked life of faith which is summed up in their drive to pray and in their lives as pray-ers.

Within days after his untimely death in 1961, friends of the United Nations General Secretary, Dag Hammarskjold, found, in his apartment, a personal diary which Hammarskjold described in a letter to a friend as a "sort of white book concerning my negotiations with myself—and with God." Written over a period of thirty-five years, this collection of reflections, aphorisms, prayers, and poems attests to a profound spiritual life based on a need for self-giving and a desire for the presence of God. Deeply influenced by his meditations on the scriptures, *The Imitation of Christ*, the writings of Meister Eckhart, John of the Cross, and, in the final years, Martin Buber, these meditations came as a surprise and shock to those who knew Hammarskjold only as a diplomat, literary person, and sophisticate. Many of the entries were keyed to important days in the liturgical calendar of the church like Christmas, New Year's Day, Good Friday, and Easter.

One entry, in particular, is germane to our discussion since it most directly touches on our subject. It comes, interestingly enough, not at the beginning of *Markings* (that title in English does not quite carry the original Swedish sense of "blaze marks" to indicate, for example, the path for hikers) but on Whitsunday in 1961, the year of his death. On that day Hammarskjold wrote:

> I don't know Who—or what—put the question. I don't know when it was put. I don't even remember answering. But at some moment I did answer Yes to Someone—or Something—and from that hour I was certain existence is meaningful and that, therefore, my life in itself had a goal.

That passage, like many in *Markings*, has a certain cryptic edge to it, but its basic outline is clear. Even the hesitation expressed in the Someone/Something indicates not intellectual confusion but that common phenomenon of mysticism in which the Sacred is beyond categorization (think of the Hindu phrase about Brahman as *neti neti*—neither this nor that). The crucial point is that the Someone/Something puts a question to which an answer is possible. There is, in short, relationship in which the presence of the Someone/Something evokes a response of yes. Furthermore, that response is not merely an acceptance of a mental conclusion. Note that Hammarskjold draws some existential conclusions from his affirmation: My existence has a meaning; in self-surrender there is a goal to be attained.

In that short entry we have encapsulated most of what we want to say about prayer as relationship: the involvement of myself and an Other; a bond that is relational; and, finally, one that touches the very core of existence and not merely its periphery. It should also be noted that in its form it is not unlike the exchanges between God and humans described in the Bible. It is true that the style of biblical description is absent, but is there that much difference between Hammarskjold's "yes" and the "yes" of Abram (Gen. 12) with which we began this chapter? In both cases is there not the revelation of God (however named), the response of the person, and the capacity to live in a radically different manner? And is there not, to press our point, relationship at the root of this exchange?

To refine our point further we might contrast the passage from Hammarskjold's *Markings* with two extraordinary incidents in the life of the French mystic Simone Weil who was a younger contemporary of Hammarskjold (he was born in 1905; she in 1908). In 1937 Simone Weil toured Italy after her unhappy experiences in the Spanish Civil War where she was scalded by boiling oil and effectively rendered useless for further service in the anti-Fascist ranks. While on a visit to Assisi, the city of Saint Francis, she visited the little Romanesque chapel of the Portiuncula (housed in an ugly baroque basilica) where, as she reported later in a letter to her friend Father Perrin, she felt compelled to go down on her knees and pray for the first time in her life. She does not tell us what the content of that prayer was or why, for the first time in her life, she felt this compulsion. She simply states it as a fact in her life.

A year later Simone Weil met a young Englishman while she was attending the Holy Week services at the famous Benedictine abbey of Solesmes in France. She had gone there with her mother mainly to hear the famous chant of the monks of the abbey. The young man introduced Simone Weil to a poem written by the metaphysical poet George Herbert with the opening lines "Love bade me welcome." She copied out the poem and formed the habit of reciting it not as a poem but in the manner of a prayer. One day while reading the poem, she says, again in a letter to Father Perrin, "Christ came down and seized me."

There is an interesting sequel to that event in Weil's life that should be mentioned because it bears on our basic thesis. Four years after the Solesmes incident Simone Weil was living in the country at the home of the lay theologian Gustave Thibon as a way of avoiding the attention of the Vichy police. She began to recite with what she called "attention" the Greek text of the Lord's Prayer. In her spiritual autobiography she tells Father Perrin that in that recitation (which brought her mystical graces) she prayed for the first time in her life. Now, in fact, she says that when she visited the Portiuncula in Assisi in the late 1930s she was "driven to her knees," and she recounts the recitation of the George Herbert poem at

Solesmes in 1938. How account for those accounts and her statement that only when she began saying the Lord's Prayer did she first begin to pray? The answer, I think, comes in distinguishing Weil's relationship to God in Christ as a basic foundation of her life from her beginning to *recite* prayers as an explicit act. In Weil's life, in short, one can see the clear distinction of being a pray-er and one who says prayers.

These two incidents, curious in their own right, are often singled out to mark the beginnings of her intense spiritual life—a life which would be at the center of her existence until she died in exile in England (she had fled with her family to escape the anti-Jewish laws of the Vichy regime in France) in 1943. What is telling about both of these incidents is that they are so characteristic of that kind of revelation which Eliade calls a *hierophany*. The power of transcendence breaks in on the soul of this young woman. That "breaking in" takes the form of a prayer (or better: the state of prayer) for this young searcher after God.

Both Simone Weil (who never was baptized as a Christian) and Dag Hammarskjold (who, while baptized, was not a conspicuous church person) focus their spiritual encounters in the person of Christ. It was Christ who "seized" Simone Weil. In the last part of the passage quoted from Hammarskjold's *Markings* he concludes with a firm christological coda: "As I continued along the Way, I learned, step by step, word by word, that behind every saying in the Gospel stands *one* man and *one* man's experience. Also behind the prayer that the cup might pass from him and his promise to drink it. Also behind each of the words from the cross."

Both Hammarskjold and Weil can be considered to be Christian outsiders. I used their stories to underscore the fact that prayer can be understood, at its most basic level, as the intimate relationship between God and the individual perceived as such. Further, I note the Christian content of these relationships because, given the subject of this book, we need to explore how prayer conceived of as relationship can be thought of in the Catholic Christian tradition. Finally, their stories are important because they were relatively free of church trappings or ecclesiastical baggage. Their conversions were stark and fundamental; in both cases it was a simple matter of response, i.e., a matter of prayer at the most fundamental level of the word.

But what about the "ordinary" Catholic? How does this schema of fundamental prayer fit into their vision of things?

Obviously, Catholic Christians pray. About that activity we will have much to say in subsequent pages. At this stage, however, we want to get behind the acts of prayer (what Heiler calls "pattern prayers") to the state of prayerfulness itself understood as a basic relationship with God.

At one level this is not a terribly difficult task. We can affirm the traditional Catholic doctrine that we are children of God in faith and through baptism, and in that condition we can call out *"Abba,* Father" (see Gal. 4:4) However, we normally think of prayer from the side of the human who speaks to God (although it is perfectly legitimate to speak of the inner life of speech of the Divine when we think of the mysterious inner life of the Trinity). Viewed from the perspective of the fundamental "yes" of the human to God we can gain, by careful analysis, a deeper appreciation of prayer as being part of the state of being faith-ful.

The very fact that we call ourselves Christians either explicitly or by gestures (like going to church) indicates, in however a confused manner, an act of affirmation. To go to church, for instance, is to say, in effect, that one affirms a relationship to God. The very gesture of going to church is both an act of faith and an act of prayer. Such acts are so unreflective, however, that they require some specificity. Otherwise the terms of the relationship between the person and God remain, at best, inchoate or unarticulated.

One fruitful approach to understanding this basic relationship might be gained by a consideration of the notion of what theologians have called the "fundamental option." Originally developed by moral theologians like Joseph Fuchs, S. J., it has served theologians to develop a more profound appreciation of the Christian life as a whole. In order to get beyond the rather mechanical understanding of sin as a punishable offense and "mortal sin" as the act(s) which lead to damnation, these theologians argue that sometime in life a person makes (or should make) a kind of basic decision about the way his or her life is to be lived. They choose, however confusedly, for a moral life as opposed to an immoral one; as believers, they choose God rather than against him. In the course of life people may do or fail to do things which are *serious* but, in their failing, they never existentially choose against God. What had been called mortal sin in the older vocabulary is, in this view of things, serious sin but it is not damnable because the fundamental option oriented toward God is not repudiated.

The point that these moral theologians strive to clarify is that many times a person may act in an imperfect manner, but in those acts there is no radical choice against God. Every person acts according to weakness but rare is the person who, in the depth of consciousness, reaches a fully accountable stage by which they say in all freedom that they choose this or that in such a way as to exclude God from their existential horizon. The fundamental option, in short, defines the stark choice of being for God or fully repudiating God.

While the concept of the fundamental option is most frequently utilized to describe the dynamics of sin, it is also a most useful notion for understanding our basic argument about prayer. People may be born into the church and raised within its culture without ever reflecting on the meaning of their faith in a deep and personal manner. Many people who have "lost their faith" have, in reality, simply cast off a way of behaving in which they have been socialized and a faith they have never assimilated in any deeply personal manner. They make a fundamental option not when they decide to remain in the church but when, in some form or another, they affirm their relationship to God in Jesus Christ. To say it another way: The fundamental option is exercised when they pray instead of merely saying prayers.

This choice may or may not be a dramatic one. Sometimes, as in the examples we have cited, it becomes a dramatic moment when, like Hammarskjold, we must utter a "yes." For most of us, the decision(s) may be ongoing, repeated, and half-understood. The basic option is to say, in some fashion or another, that I am not fully alone or fully autonomous. There is another pole to my life that cannot be fully understood, completely grasped, or entirely reached. For the Christian there is the added fact that Jesus is seen as the one who can best show us how to affirm—utter the "yes"—to that unnamed reality. In our pilgrimage to discern our relationship to the Other, we simultaneously slough off a sense of our own absolute autonomy and surrender to that larger reality which is God.

We should understand that fundamental option not as single act but as process. By making the choice we affirm that there is relationship. In that affirmation the life of prayer has already begun. Our more conventional understanding of prayer may then be understood as giving voice to the choice/option we have already made. Again, and we will argue this at some length throughout this book, that giving voice to our choice for God may range from the merely perfunctory ("saying our prayers") to the profoundly personal moments of affective communion with God. The point that needs emphasis is that all prayer roots itself in that willingness to choose for God. When that choice has been made we affirm the Other, and by that fact we are pray-ers.

In an extremely interesting article in the *Summa* Saint Thomas argues (in II IIae q. 83 a. 10) that prayer is proper to human beings and not found either in the divine persons of the Trinity (who are equal) or in the lower animals who lack reason. While it is true, Thomas says, that the scriptures depict God as hearing the cries of the young ravens for food (see Ps. 147:9) this means only that all things have a natural order oriented back to God precisely because they are creatures. Humans alone, he argues, can understand that they stand in relationship to God and, in that understanding, possess both the right and the obligation to pray.

Past generations of Thomists have taught us to appreciate how dynamically Thomas conceived reason to be. As intellectual creatures we have a basic dynamism toward knowing and loving. When Thomas argues that prayer is peculiar to humans he is saying, by that fact, that prayer is part of the human constitution. This is an insight that goes back at least as far as Augustine's famous formulation in the *Confessions* that God has created us for himself and we are restless until we rest in him. The proper end of human life, in that reading of the matter, is that we are called, in our humanity, to be pray-ers.

It is in Saint Augustine's *Confessions* that we find the clearest statement of the thesis we have argued in this chapter. The very title of Augustine's book admits of at least two meanings: It is a confession of Augustine's sinfulness but, further, it is a confession of his faith in God. That is why Augustine casts so much of the book in the form of direct address to God. In one sense, the *Confessions* can be seen as an extended prayer of praise.

The first six sections of book one of the *Confessions* can be viewed as a prelude or introduction to the whole. It is noteworthy to see that Augustine begins this prelude by asking a simple and direct question: Can one pray to God before knowing him or must one first know God (in faith) before prayer is possible? Augustine answers that question not by affirming the priority of faith over prayer or vice versa but by noting the inextricable relationship of the two: "I shall look for you, Lord, by praying to you and as I pray, I shall believe in you" (I.1).

That, in a nutshell, is the whole matter. While, at first glance, it seems abstruse and speculative, in reality the intimate connection between being a believer (or seeking to be one) and being a pray-er is obvious to anyone on the faith journey. To affirm God in faith is rarely reducible to a simple intellectual declaration that there might be a supreme reality. People seek out God because they desire to have some absolute wholeness to their lives, some horizon against which their lives make some sort of sense. It is a matter not of intellectual satisfaction but of deep existential need.

If people feel that they stand in such a relation they will say so to themselves and make a gesture to affirm it. This affirmative act is, simultaneously, faith and prayer. That is why within the life and practice of the faith community acts of faith are also juxtaposed to prayer. In the liturgy we listen to the readings from scripture but end those readings with prayer responses. That is why, further, after the consecration of the eucharistic elements we say in unison an acclamation of faith. That is why, finally, there is a postcommunion prayer. The action of the liturgy is, simultaneously, a gesture of faith and an act of prayer. We come to those celebrations both in faith and in prayer. Those moments are not easily separable.

While the close conjunction of being a person of faith and a person of prayer is, at a certain level, a commonplace, it is nonetheless one of those commonplaces that bear examination because of the implications that can be drawn from it. Many people find it difficult to consider themselves persons of prayer. They well might say prayers but, for many and varied reasons, they may well consider the condition of being a prayer only possible for those religious virtuosi one reads about in hagiography and church history. The idea of constant prayer or passing long hours in prayer seems fine for a Saint Francis on Mt. Alverno (or Jesus in the Garden of Gethsemane), but it does not seem like a realistic part of one's ordinary life.

Now it is true that history gives us examples of virtuosi of prayer, and it is likewise true that certain others of a keen sensibility are driven to prayer in explicit and dramatic ways. Most of us, however, might punctuate our lives by moments of prayer (in the morning, at Mass, etc.) but do not consider our lives anchored in prayer in any explicit manner. We see ourselves as very much occasional or episodic in "raising the heart and mind of God."

The conviction that this book wants to drive home is that a person who has made a choice for faith, an option for God, or a surrender to faith is already a person of prayer. Prior to the formal gestures of "naming" that choice or option or surrender, there is already present in life the *condition* of prayer. The great task of Christian growth is to give awareness to that fundamental condition in an explicit and consistent manner.

This sense of life as being in a condition of prayer when it is a life of faith also helps us to hold firm to the absolute mystery which is God. It has been one of the conspicuous merits of modern theologians like Paul Tillich and Karl Rahner to disabuse us of the idea that God is one more being in the universe, albeit the greatest Being. Properly speaking, says Tillich, God does not exist in the sense of "standing out" as a Being among other beings. God is the ground and foundation and horizon of all being(s) in the created universe. Again, and this is Rahner's formulation of it, long before we can give flesh and substance to the notion of God we start from the absolute mystery which is under and beyond our limited lives. We are, to say it another way, confronted by the absolute mystery that stands behind all creation, and only then do we begin to name that mystery as God or Father. To turn that observation into our particular angle of vision is to say that first we stand in the mystery of God and then we name it; we are in faith as pray-ers, and only then do we formulate our faith and begin to pray.

It is interesting to note that Paul Tillich discusses prayer in his *Systematic Theology* in relationship to the doctrine of the providence of God. Tillich argues for the validity of the prayer of petition because he sees such utterances as acts of human freedom by which we attempt to reconcile our lives with what Tillich calls the "directing creativity" of God. In other words, when we say "give us this day our daily bread" we are uttering words which give shape to the prior faith that the particulars and generalities of human existence are within the care of God. As such, prayer is not an act of magical manipulation; it is, rather, the act of making explicit our convictions of being within God. It is, as it were, to name our condition as believers under God's care.

Prayer harkens back to faith and faith brings forth prayer. Nowhere is that more clearly illustrated than in an incident recorded in the Gospel of Saint Mark (9:14ff.). A boy who has an unclean spirit is brought to Jesus. The disciples had failed to exorcise the spirit. The boy's father begs Jesus to have pity and help his son. Jesus says that all things are possible to one who believes. The man cries out, "I believe, Lord. Help my unbelief" (v. 24). Let us recall the unfolding of the story. The man approaches Jesus in faith who inquires about its strength. The man confesses his faith and, simultaneously, asks for an increase of it. His cry is both a confession of faith and a prayer for faith and help. It is to the dual profession that Jesus responds. When, later in the story, he tells the disciples that such exorcisms can be driven out only by prayer (v. 29), he refers not only to his own relationship to God (which is not alluded to in the text) but to that powerful cry of faith uttered by the man who, simultaneously, pays tribute to the power of Christ and his ability to answer his need. Faith and prayer, in that Gospel narrative, intertwine and touch each other in a way that were either element missing, the other would lack meaning. What is true of that narrative is true of the Christian life as a whole.

A Prayer

Give me great seriousness in all that concerns faith.
Teach me to see what it needs to exist and be fruitful.
Let me know its strength but also its weakness.
If with the passing of time my feeling should change, and with it the human form though not the divine content of my faith, then teach me to understand this change.
Grant that in the tests that it will bring I may stand firm, so that my faith may constantly gain stature and maturity as you, O ruler of all life, have so ordained it.
Amen.

Romano Guardini (1885–1968) was one of the most prolific and influential theologians of this century. Born in Verona, he was a lifelong resident of Germany where he had a distinguished academic career. He wrote on theology, liturgy, and literature. From 1948 until his retirement in 1963, he held the chair of philosophy of religion and the Catholic worldview at Munich (a similar position at the University of Berlin had been abolished by the Nazis in 1939). At his retirement, the chair was assumed by the late Karl Rahner.

At the conclusion of his public theological lectures Guardini customarily recited a prayer composed by himself for the particular occasion of the lecture. Guardini eventually collected these prayers and published them under the title *Theologisches Gebete;* they appeared in English in a fine little volume, *Prayers from Theology* (New York: Herder and

Herder, 1959). It is from that volume that the above prayer is excerpted.

In a sense Guardini's prayer sets my thesis on its head: He begins with the fragility of our faith and prays for its enrichment in "stature and maturity." The hidden subtext, however, and this is our thesis boldly stated, is that Guardini can pray for faith and its maturation because only in faith can he pray; the one presupposes, and gives texture to, the other.

A Note on Readings

Mircea Eliade's *The Sacred and the Profane* (New York: Harcourt, 1957) can be supplemented by his *Patterns in Comparative Religion* (New York: Sheed and Ward, 1958); both books treat his basic idea of religiousness as a "mode of being." Periodic reviews of Eliade's ideas and publications, along with abundant bibliographies, are included in the essay by Seymour Cain, "Mircea Eliade's Attitudes toward History," *Religious Studies Review* 6 (January 1980), pp. 13–16, and the reviews by Ilinca Johnston, Lawrence Sullivan, and James Buchanan in *Religious Studies Review* 9 (January 1983), pp. 11–23.

William James's *The Varieties of Religious Experience* in the recent edition edited by Frederick Burkhardt and Fredson Bowers (Cambridge, MA: Harvard University Press, 1985) is now the best and most exhaustively annotated version available. Friedrich Heiler's *Prayer: A Study in the History and Psychology of Religion* (New York: Oxford University Press, 1932) is, alas, long out of print. Rudolph Otto's *The Idea of the Holy* (New York: Oxford University Press, 1958) is often reprinted.

For a recent survey of books on prayer, see Lawrence S. Cunningham, "Meanings and Methods of Prayer," *Church* (Summer 1988), pp. 47–50.

The most readable translation of Pascal's *Pensées* that I have found is that of A. J. Krailsheimer in the Penguin series (Harmondsworth and Baltimore, 1966). Jean Mesnard's *Pascal* (University, AL: University of Alabama Press, 1969) has been a handy and readable vade mecum to the text itself.

Leif Sjoberg and W. H. Auden translated Dag Hammarskjold's *Markings* (New York: Knopf, 1964) with Auden also supplying the introduction. His remarks should be read in the light of two more sophisticated interpretations of Hammarskjold's book: Henry P. Van Dusen's *Dag Hammarskjold: The Man and His Faith* (New York: Harper and Row, rev. ed., 1969) and Gustaf Aulen's *Dag Hammarskjold's White Book: The Meanings of Markings* (Philadelphia: Fortress, 1969).

The autobiographical essays of Simone Weil are found in *Waiting for God*, translated by Emma Craufurd (New York: Harper and Row, 1973; original edition, 1951). For background, see Simone Petremont, *Simone Weil: A Life*, translated by Raymond Rosenthal (New York: Random House, 1976).

Josef Fuchs's notion of the fundamental option is developed in his *Human Values and Christian Morality* (Dublin: Gill, 1977). The balance between the fundamental option and accountability for personal acts is a delicate one. That relationship was one subject of discussion between the Reverend Charles Curran and the Sacred Congregation for the Doctrine of the Faith; see Charles Curran, *Faithful Dissent* (Kansas City, MO: Sheed and Ward, 1986), pp. 176ff. Curran cites Fuchs as well as Bernard Häring's *Free and Faithful in Christ: Moral Theology for Clergy and Laity*, vol. 1 (New York: Seabury, 1978), and Sean Fagan's *Has Sin Changed?* (Wilmington, DE: Glazier, 1977) for further discussions of the fundamental option.

R. S. Pine-Coffin's translation of the *Confessions* for Penguin Books (Harmondsworth and Baltimore, 1961) is extremely readable. I gained much from reading Robert O'Connell's *St. Augustine's Confessions: The Odyssey of Soul* (Cambridge, MA: Belknap Press of Harvard University, 1969) as well as the recent symposium on the *Confessions* in the *Journal of the Scientific Study of Religion* (March 1986), pp. 57–115. For a general survey of our topic, see Gervase Corcoran, "Saint Augustine on Prayer," *Augustinian Heritage* 34 (1988), pp. 203–16.

Karl Rahner is never simple, but a careful reading of his *Foundations of Christian Faith*, translated by William V. Dych

(New York: Crossroad, 1978) pays immense rewards. For Paul Tillich I have used his three-volume (bound as one) *Systematic Theology* (Chicago: University of Chicago Press, 1967).

There is a profile of Romano Guardini as a theologian in *Theologians of Our Time*, edited by Leonard Reisisch (South Bend, IN: Notre Dame University Press, 1964), pp. 109–26.

2

WORDS

*When one speaks lovingly of God, all
human words are like blind lions searching for
a spring in the desert.*

Leon Bloy

If prayer is relationship, as we have argued, we can say
that this relationship demands to be expressed in one form or
another. While it is quite true that many relationships, even
deep and intimate ones, exist without expression—as pure
presence—they never do so for extended, much less perma-
nent, periods of time. Creation itself—the pure relation of
creator to creation—is, according to the scriptures, the gift of
articulation: In the beginning was the Word.

Similarly, the nexus between believer and God, while a basic and sustaining relationship, always finds expression and
enunciation. It is essential to being human to express what
one is and how one stands in the world. To be deprived of
language, to be incapable of stating who one is, is to be condemned to the most devastating form of autism. The cruelest
pain of autism, after all, is that the person afflicted cannot
break out to others while others cannot connect with the one
afflicted. It is not a poetic cliché to say that no person is an
island; for when one is an island, one is most cruelly bur-
dened. It is a plain and irreducible fact of human life that we
created "our" world through the medium of language and
without language there is no world. That is as true of the
quotidian world as it is of the world of faith.

28

If one stands before the unutterable mystery which is God it is inevitable that one will "say," first to the self, and then to others, what that relation is and attempt to say what it means. This saying is never generic. It is always a "saying" in which the available resources of one's education, culture, and intelligence play their part. If the relationship of a person to God is really experienced (rather than just "thought about") there will be powerful demands put on language to convey the encounter with that mystery. That, I think, is what T. S. Eliot had in mind when he lamented about words which "strain,/ Crack and sometimes break, under the burden,/ Under the tension" (*Four Quartets*).

The problem of language is compounded when one speaks to oneself about the mystery of God and to others and, further, when one speaks back to God. God is not perceived in the Christian tradition as some Void beyond naming but as gracious mystery who, while inadequately named can, nonetheless, be addressed. God is there (and here) as the basic context for my being long before God is addressed, but even in that presence he is called upon: "Even before a word is upon my tongue, lo, O Lord, thou knowest it altogether" (Ps. 139:4). In the encounter with God we speak to God even though God knows us prior to that speech. Indeed, it is part of the mystery of grace, as Karl Rahner insists over and over, that the very capacity to speak to God comes, not from our efforts, but from the grace-fulness of God who first prompts us.

To speak of the relationship of words to authentic prayer we need to distinguish some basically different ways in which prayer becomes speech. First, there are those personal articulations that derive subjectively from our experience of the mystery of God. Secondly, there is the appropriation of prayers that, by reason of their place in a tradition, invite us to join our voices to theirs. Finally, there is that prayer which is more than traditional because it is the one that Jesus invites us to use: the Lord's Prayer. We need to say some words about each kind of prayer as speech.

We must start with the surge of words that comes out from a person who actually lives in relationship with God. My contention is that this articulation of relationship bears a strong relationship to the creation of poetry. This thesis is stated despite the fact that the particular relationship between poetry and prayer is a vexatious one which has exercised extremely astute writers in this century, ranging from Henri Brémond and the Maritains to E. I. Watkin, Louis Martz, and others (see the partial reading list at the end of this chapter). My purpose is not to enter into those complex theoretical discussions, although I have profited from reading them. My starting point is a good deal more modest.

When speaking of poetry I do not mean the technical act of creating or making (poesis) a piece of literature but that poetic impulse which demands that a particular emotion or human reaction can have its surplus of meaning condensed into an utterable whole. That, I think, is what the true poet manages to do rarely with full success but attempts to do every time he or she begins to write a poem. The test I have often proposed to my students runs something like this: Think of the happiest moment of your life (or, if one is a pessimist, the most miserable moment) and try to convey that moment in all of its texture and nuance to someone else in a limited number of words. Such a "conveyance" is what James Joyce had in mind when he made his famous analogy (in A Portrait of the Artist as a Young Man) between the poet and the priest at Mass: The poet, in writing, "transubstantiates" the gross material of the world by uttering effective and transforming words. Words, in a very real sense of the term, can change the world and the way we insert ourselves into it.

Interestingly enough, Karl Rahner makes very much the same point from a somewhat different angle of vision. In an essay entitled "Priest and Poet," Rahner appeals to what he calls "primordial words" (Urwortes) whose use provides a door that opens into the unfathomable depths of true reality. The poet, like the priest, utters those words not in a scattered and uninformed manner but in what Rahner calls a "powerful concentration." In that calling forth of the primordial words, language brings forth the fundamental beauty of reality that stands in front of the unutterable mystery which is God. It is easy to see what Rahner means when we think of the deep power of words in the sacramental life of the church. Words forgive, heal, communicate, transubstantiate, and bind. Furthermore, some words in the religious tradition are so fundamental that any attempt to paraphase them fails. What, for example, could we say that would supplant those signs of gross materiality which stands behind our sacramental life: bread, water, wine, oil . . . ? Those signs take on a full and concentrated meaning precisely because the traditional words that accompany them have accumulated so much significance over their centuries of use.

If sacred language is authentic, that is, if it really expresses the deep relationship between the believer and God, it is going to be a language which somehow attempts to do justice to that relationship. That is why the psychologist-theologians Barry and Ann Ulanov can call prayer a form of "primary speech" that speaks not only of the reality of God but about whom one is and how he or she stands in the world. Their notion of "primary speech" is very close to Martin Buber's concept of primary relationship. Buber's classic work *I and Thou* is founded on the notion that the most authentic bond for a human is in his/her capacity to utter a "thou" to another. When one does that in the encounter with the very mystery of existence one is, simultaneously, addressing the Eternal Thou who is God. In that relationship one does not encapsulate God in speech; rather, one addresses God. That is, in Buber's understanding, both primary relationship and primary speech. It expresses that bond which makes us, in one and the same act, believers and pray-ers.

One often sees scenes in movies where the hero/heroine, caught in a seemingly impossible situation, turns to prayer with an introduction that expresses not faith but doubt: "Look, I don't know if You are up there or if You hear us, but if you do I'd like to ask for the life of this little girl, etc., etc." Such scenes are, inevitably, banal and cliché-ridden, but they do carry with them an insight: Before deep prayer, born from need, gets said there is some prior need to establish, however tenuously, a sense of relationship. It is only when that sense of relationship exists that it becomes possible to utter the "right" words or to express the appropriate sentiments in words. Again, to return to our hypothetical movie scene, there is a compulsion to affirm a kind of doubt that can mean either (a) that the person was not much of a believer, or (b) that a person feels a certain sense of unworthiness or reluctance to turn to God in prayer. Interestingly enough (all clichés bring with them homely truths!) such protestations carry the seed of that genuine humility which is at the root of authentic prayer.

When a person gives voice to that sense of being related to Something Else they are, in effect, doing exactly the same thing as the poet even if they would not consider themselves "poetical" in any ordinary sense of the term. It also explains why the great virtuosi of the spiritual life have such a characteristic approach to language, whether it be in the ecstatic utterance of pure poetry (Saint Francis of Assisi), the extended use of paradox and metaphor (Saints Teresa of Avila and John of the Cross), or the creation of a new and puzzling vocabulary obscure in its daring attempt to capture that which is beyond naming (Meister Eckhart). What the language of the great masters and mistresses of prayer always teaches us is that an authentic sense of the living reality of God, when expressed in human language, is going to stretch that language in new and, often, uncharted ways. It is that constant search for a pure and authentic language in deep prayer that makes prayer a genuine source for theological meditation. Ordinary language, in short, suffices for prayer and yet does not suffice, if only because it never approaches the limit of what we want to express.

Indeed, the very fact that God has no name (see Exod. 3) creates a paradox. For the mystics, the journey begins in words and ends in silence. The very attempt to name and articulate the *experience* (for the mystical it is, after all, an experience, not an "idea") of the Other which is God demonstrates, at one and the same time, that language points us to but never does justice to God's reality. The very failure of language spoken before the mystery of God is only a failure of language; it is, simultaneously, an affirmation of the reality which is beyond the powers of human articulation. That is why there is profound truth in Martin Buber's famous assertion that God can never be expressed, only addressed. Behind Buber's aphorism, after all, is his very real fear of those who would identify their concept of God—their expression of God—with the reality of the Eternal Thou. It also explains why the tradition that emphasizes words in prayer (e.g., the Jesus Prayer, the tradition of the *Cloud of Unknowing*) also emphasizes that words should be "let go" when the presence of God is experienced. Words are only a vehicle to that one who is in essence, Word.

There comes a time in the life of prayer (the mystics testify to this) when words can cease—at least for a moment—and all that remains is presence. Hence, following on what we have said up to this point we note a kind of fugal relationship in the life of prayer: We make an option for a relationship with God. We give that option utterance in prayer. In that utterance we can, at times, stop "saying" and simply be. Saint Bonaventure, in the end of *The Mind's Journey* calls this stage a kind of death and concludes his journey to God by saying that we should die and impose silence on our cares; we can then say, with Philip in the Gospel, "It is enough for us" (see John 14:8). It is also why, in a more contemporary mode, Thomas Merton could write a friend, in a rare autobiographical statement about his own life of prayer, that his prayer was best understood as attention before the presence of God, a kind of praise "rising up out of the center of Nothing and Silence."

For most of us, however, the strain to create a new language or even to surpass the language that we do use in prayer is not an urgent problem. When we stand before God, either privately or in community, we most likely rely on those words that have been part and parcel of our upbringing and our culture. This is as it should be, since few of us create a private language; we inherit and shape the one that is characteristic of our community and its milieu. This is true of language in general and the language of prayer in particular.

Every religion is, almost by definition, conservative. What constitutes a religion in history is its fierce protectiveness about its story (hence the process by which a canon is created) and ways in which that story becomes ritualized in liturgy or its analogues. Nothing can create a schism faster in a religious tradition than attempts to tamper with the received tradition of religious language. One does not have to go to ancient history to see that. Every week on the religious page of any local newspaper there are advertisements for Episcopal churches that use only the 1928 Prayerbook or Independent Baptist churches which assure people that they read only the King James Version of the Bible and traditionalist Roman Catholic churches that advertise Masses according to the "Tridentine rite." While such positions are often seen as eruptions of fanaticism (think of the sanguinary repression of the Old Believers in Russia over matters of minor liturgical practice), the fact is such struggles attest that for many believers words must be the "right" ones precisely because words reflect what is real. "Wrong" words create not mere linguistic dissonance; they cut to the heart of what is true. The history of any religious tradition is very much a history of the conservation of hallowed prayers. As long as a religious tradition has vitality, attempts to satirize or mock religious language carries with it an edge of blasphemy or sacrilege. There is no community that would cry out against the misuse of prayers offered to Zeus, but similar misuse directed at the Gospel or the Torah or the Qur'an would bring down the wrath of both believers and of those who still feel a respect for those who are believers.

There is a further point. We may come to faith and, in the words of that faith, wish to address God. We do not exist in a total cultural or linguistic void. When we wish to reach out in language to God it is both inevitable and natural that we should do so from the accumulated language of our own tradition. Even those who do not pray know the conventions of prayer. They can imitate—or parody—the language of "thee" and "thou" with ease. We have at our disposal an entire vocabulary of prayer with which to start. It is only in the actual articulation of prayer that we begin to sift and choose that language which most appropriately connects to our own experience of faith.

Raised in a religious tradition like Catholicism we learn, at an early age, certain prayers or prayer phrases that, over the course of time, have been "canonized" by use and tradition. Often we learn these prayers long before we understand them. For years I said, in the Act of Contrition, that I was "hardly sorry" for all my sins, since "heartily" was not part of my mental or actual vocabulary. At this level such prayers have a talismanic function. They are said because they are the formulae that indicate who we are. That is why there is a Catholic as well as a Protestant formula for grace before meals. That is why, further, that when asked to pray, a Catholic will almost by instinct make the sign of the cross. That simple prayer-gesture "frames," as it were, the beginning and the end of the language of prayer.

When—and who knows precisely when this occurs?—we begin to reflect on the words we have uttered as part of our upbringing we then begin to face the issue of meaning and personal significance. The cadences of words, the settings in which they are uttered (before meals, upon retiring, before Mass, etc.) now give way to more urgent issues: Am I, in fact, heartily sorry or hardly sorry? Are we, in fact, receiving this food "from thy bounty"? That questioning arises either through the natural process of growth and intellectual curiosity or, not infrequently, through crisis. Who can forget that powerful moment in Elie Wiesel's *Night* when, in the midst of the Yom Kippur service at Auschwitz, the young boy cries out in the silence of his heart: "Why should I bless his holy name?" It is at those moments that the intersection of prayer and personal commitment comes to the fore with a demand for clarity and resolution.

To put the matter in a somewhat different form: When the utterance of prayer is conjoined to the instinct for reflection and the question of meaning, theology is being done at the most basic level. That is what the old monastic writer Evagrius of Pontus meant when he wrote that the person who truly prayed was a *theologos* and, conversely, only the *theologos* knew how to pray adequately.

The reflective encounter with the words of prayer inevitably brings us either to a new-found skepticism or to an urgent need to deepen and rephrase in our own heads what these words might possibly mean *for us*. In the former case it may be that we cannot any longer say certain words (how many adults can say "Angel of God, my guardian dear, to whom God's love," etc.?) because of the growth of our personal horizon or because, more fundamentally, the words do not reflect in any real sense who we are or what we stand for. It may even be that the words create a dissonance that we cannot overcome. In such circumstances we sense discord between what we say and who we are. Was that not the dilemma of Claudius in the prayer scene of *Hamlet*? Claudius had the problem not of skepticism but of belief. It was precisely because he feared the just retribution of God that he could not bend his "stubborn knee." His prayers mocked his true desires and intentions. His words ascended but his thoughts stayed below; words, Claudius knew, without thoughts "scarce to heaven go."

Furthermore, the relationship of our being pray-ers and the words of prayer is problematic not only when there is dissonance about who we are in terms of age or moral condition. For the believer who enters into the tradition of prayer there is the simple problem of the overuse of words: their familiarity. The case of the recitation of the Lord's Prayer is a case in point. All Catholics learn that prayer in early childhood. The occasions for its recitation are numerous either through prescription (so many times in the saying of the rosary, once at every Mass, as a penance after confession, etc.) or through the personal structure of our spiritual lives by the choice of that prayer in the morning or evening or as a "starter" for meetings, Bible study, etc.

To compute the actual number of times that a typical Catholic has said that prayer would be a mind-boggling exercise. That number, whatever it might be, should be juxtaposed with the commonplace observation issued by all the patristic commentators that we should say this prayer only with the boldness (*parrhesia*) that comes from grace. The Lord's Prayer, coming as it does from the very lips of Christ, has been traditionally seen as the wellspring of the human relationship with God. Thus Maximus the Confessor, in his introduction to a commentary on the prayer, says that it "contains in outline, mysteriously hidden, or to speak more properly, openly proclaimed for all those whose understanding is strong enough, the whole scope of what the words deal with." Seven centuries later Saint Thomas Aquinas would make essentially the same point when, in the *Summa* (II IIae q. 83 a. 9) he would argue that the prayer is the most perfect of prayers because it contains within it everything that a human could desire while ordering all those desires properly. It is a prayer, after all, that comes from divine revelation and from the mouth of Christ.

Now the question occurs: How often has anyone said the Lord's Prayer with anything like the attention that the entire theological tradition demands? How often has the typical Catholic (how often have I?) "dared" to say the Lord's Prayer despite the fact that in the old liturgy we were warned to do so: *audemus dicere*—"we dare to say"? More than likely, we say "Our Father" because it is there as a given in the liturgy or part of the structure of the common devotional life that is equally given. It is not that we disbelieve the words of the prayer; it is that we are not often reflective enough to consider what we are saying.

Conversely, one could say that precisely because the Lord's Prayer has attained the status of a classic (I am thinking of David Tracy's understanding of the theological classic), it can be situated easily in the liturgy as a form of common prayer or as the locus for intensive private prayer. The history of spirituality gives ample testimony to both uses. The fact that people go back to that prayer to wring new meanings from it indicates that the words of the prayer allow for an inexhaustible range of meanings and resonances. Indeed, some of the early commentators, like Tertullian and Origen, saw the Lord's Prayer as an "outline of prayer" which we could fill in both by the addition of our petitions and by deepening our understanding of what we were saying. It may well be that in the saying of the Lord's Prayer we simply pray in a conventional manner without plumbing the possibility of the words. At that level of prayer the words have not yet taken on a strong conceptual meaning in our life of faith which the commentary tradition insists we must learn if we are to understand the prayer at all.

Such lack of reflection does not mean, of necessity, superstition, hypocrisy, or sheer routine. Pattern words drop from our lips in a constant stream as part of our daily routine ("Have a nice day!") with a minimal amount of attention. Such verbal gestures have their power, such as it is, not through our reflections on them but in our readiness to use them rather than their opposite ("Have a rotten day!"). The fact that we say the Lord's Prayer in the morning or evening or at the liturgy means, at a very minimum, that we still identify ourselves as capable or willing to affirm a religious sentiment that invokes Someone beyond ourselves. At that level, at least, the saying of prayers goes beyond the talismanic to become, however imperfectly, an act of faith. It is that very basic truth that we should keep in mind before we are quick to condemn those who "say" prayers in an unmindful or nonreflective way.

Actually to focus attention, in a sustained way, on the words of prayer may require some reflection either as innocent as curiosity (is God really a Shepherd or a Father and in what sense?) or as compelling as a crisis of faith (why am I saying these words?) or as a response to a religious impulse to deepen our commitment to the words we say in an effort to strengthen the life of prayer. It is an old spiritual strategy, mentioned in most of the manuals of meditation or treatises on prayer, to use the formulae of prayers as points or moments of meditation: to say prayers prayerfully. The roots of that practice go back at least as far as the monastic *lectio divina* and enjoy a new appeal with the popularity of the practice known as "centering prayer." At the heart of this tradition is the practice of appropriating word(s) in a deep and contemplative manner.

The fact that we "know" a number of prayers and recite them with regularity might never provide us with a sense of their power until the words are ripped from their familiar setting and face us either as a challenge to our complacency or as an anchorhold to be grasped in times of great trial.

It is quite easy, for instance, to say "thy will be done" when things go swimmingly along in their expected ordinariness. The words take on an urgent thickness, however, when we are faced with a real crisis or tragedy and then must say "thy will be done" when what is in our hearts is not submission but despair or rebellion.

The distinction that Paul Ricoeur has made famous between "first naïveté" and "second naïveté" may be helpful in this regard. As children, for example, we may have read the Nativity story of Luke or Matthew with a naïve vision of ascending and descending angels, choirs in the heavens, and so on. When we penetrate the biblical text more deeply, those images may leave us for a plateau of second naïveté where we begin to attend to the deeper and more existentially satisfying strands of the narratives. So it is with our approach to prayer. There comes a time when we can turn back to the prayers of our tradition to see them in a new light and with a deeper appreciation of their significance (or it may happen that we simply outgrow them). There comes a time, in short, where "Father" can no longer mean a bigger-than-life patriarch for us. There comes a time when the full significance of the "*Abba*" experience of Jesus takes on new and thicker resonances in our life of faith.

On the other hand, there may come a time when the words of prayer are the only thing that is left to us; they become the anchors of reality. That point is strikingly made in Iris Murdoch's powerful novel *The Good Apprentice* (1986). Edward, the hero of the novel, causes the death of his good friend through a combination of callousness and innocent stupidity. The death causes Edward to fall into a black pit of personal despair that renders him almost helpless. In a conversation with his half-brother he tries to explain his despair, which is exacerbated by the accusatory letters he receives from his dead friend's mother. Stuart, the half-brother, begs him to dare to hope. He says to him with great urgency:

> Try to sort of pray, say "deliver me from evil," say you're sorry, ask for help, it will come; it must come, find some light, something the blackness cannot blacken. There must be things you have, things you can get to, some poetry, something from the bible, Christ if he still means anything to you. Let the pain go on but let something else touch it like a ray coming through from outside, from that place outside.

In both the instances we have just cited, the common thread is that the words of prayer can take on deep meaning when they are removed from their familiar setting and given an urgent life of their own within the context of a life or my life. It is precisely that close connection between the urgency of life and the authenticity of words which gives a particular edge to the prayers of Jesus. The *"Abba* experience" of Jesus, often cited by scholars as the very core of his religious sensibility, is reflected not only in the familiar address of God as Father, but also in those prayers that the New Testament records as being at the core of his relationship to God.

Such prayers of Jesus cluster naturally enough in the accounts of his passion and death. It is in this dramatic setting that Jesus is able to give expression to the basic consonance between his will and that of God. It is worthy of note, I think, that the passion narratives are framed with intensely personal prayer. When Jesus goes to the Garden of Gethsemane, just before his betrayal, he cries out his *"Abba-*Father" asking for the cup to be passed from him but quickly adding that it is the *Abba's* will not his that should be done. (See Mark 14:36; Matt. 26:39 which says "My Father" and Luke 22:42 with simply "Father.") The unfolding of the Father's will reaches its culmination on the cross where Jesus accepts (and sactifies) the ultimate human experience of death with the completion of the Gethsemane prayer: He cries out in a loud voice (Matt. 27:50; Mark 15:37) "Father, into thy hands I commend my spirit" (Luke 23:46).

Those paradigmatic prayers, rooted in the experience of Jesus, derive from the inner urgency and consistency of authentic bonds between Jesus and the Father; they are not merely the contrivances of the artificer of words. That these words are remembered in the scriptures and proclaimed in the assembly of the church is a salutary reminder that it is through the agency of those prayers that we come to some intuition of the *Abba* faith which was that of Jesus and, by extension, that which should be ours.

There is a further point. The prayers of Jesus that we have mentioned above are precisely right for the occasions in which they are uttered. The anticipation of the passion in the

Garden and the last moments on the cross provide a fitting setting for the cry of Jesus to the *Abba*-Father. They are unique and unrepeatable moments. Further, they are moments that are not ritualized or stylized. They derive from the exigent moments of a life as it unfolds in all of its drama. We need to remember this because we so often think about those prayers of Jesus not as coming from moments of life but as "records" enshrined in the written Gospels or, as in the case of the Last Words of Jesus, stylized in oratorio performances or dramatic presentations in the Holy Week liturgy.

That tension between prayer in a life situation and in a stylized setting is not dissimilar from the ways in which the words of prayer occur in our own lives. Quite frequently we say the words of prayer in an expected and sanctioned setting (e.g., before meals in the family; in church as part of the liturgy). The words "fit" there not so much because they have a peculiar meaning but because they seem to be comfortable in that setting. The proof of that can be seen by trying to imagine what it would be like to say those same words, say, in the middle of a shopping mall or, sotto voce, in the midst of a cocktail party or sporting event. Quite bluntly, the idea would probably never even occur to us; the setting is not right.

The setting does become right, however, when we abandon the formulaic prayers for those prayers that well up from deep need or as an almost automatic reaction to a situation. It might never occur to us to say the Lord's Prayer while in the bleachers at a ball game, but it would seem quite natural to say, on seeing a stricken and immobile player on the field, "Please God, do not let him be seriously hurt."

For everything there is a place and time. Formal prayer deserves its setting (we shall say much more about this in the pages on the liturgy), and spontaneous prayer will find its outlet. At this point what we wish to underscore are the diverse patterns in which the words of prayer find their apt place of articulation. Furthermore, we would like to argue that, while formulaic prayers have a formal and accustomed setting, their meaning is not exhausted by those constrictions of time and place. Indeed, we would insist that were we to form the habit of reflecting on the meaning of those prayers and the significance of the words in which they find expression, we can arrive at a deeper sense of their meaning and provide ourselves with an entry into a more profound relationship with God.

The unspoken assumption here is that the classic prayers of the Catholic tradition—the Lord's Prayer, the Ave Maria, etc.—have not exhausted their usefulness precisely because they remain in the tradition, give witness to its historicity, and are invoked in the very act of affirming that tradition. Such prayers, as it were, "frame" our lives as believers and as members of a faith community. We recite such prayers both because their authenticity is guaranteed by the tradition and because they "fit" the life we have assumed. We also understand their validity, it might be noted in passing, when we hear those words parodied or put to profane or humorous use. We resist such parodies because the words have meaning for us. We would not bristle, for example, if someone were to parody an ode in honor of Zeus or Hera.

Those prayers that well up from some dramatic situation, by contrast, have less to do with our inherited tradition and more to do with our situation as radically contigent beings. We cry out in such moments precisely because all of the possible means of sustenance seem impotent or absent. Such prayers are also embedded in the formal worship of the church, but we rarely reflect on their presence; they have become stylized and domesticated through use. When, for instance, we say in unison "Lord, have mercy!" in response to the petitions at the beginning of the liturgy, it is rarely that we think of such a recitation as a cry for help for those being named. That, however, is precisely the dynamic behind those prayers.

It would not be fair to conclude that such prayers lack honesty or power. All it means is that when the words of prayer take on a certain formality, that brings with it a familarity not breeding contempt but lack of reflection. Were we to reflect on it we would all agree that we would like God to "forgive us our trespasses" just as we would wish God to "have mercy" on us and those for whom we pray or to "grant us peace in our day."

The issue, baldly stated, is that the words of prayer, except in those relatively rare crisis moments when they well up out of deep need and conviction, need to be recovered through reflection and vigilance. The challenge of prayer is, in short, to wed meaning to utterance. It is precisely for this reason that the split between vocal prayer and mental prayer (or liturgy and contemplation) is a tendentious one. It may well be that we at times speak in prayer without conscious reflection. But such prayers, uttered for the mere sake of utterance, have never been an ideal in the life of prayer. Indeed, in Matthew's account Jesus warns against such prayer as a prelude to his utterance of the Lord's Prayer: "And in praying do not heap up empty phrases as the Gentiles do; for they think they will be heard for their many words" (Matt. 6:7). While it may be true, as we have argued, that the "saying" of prayers can reflect an act of faith by the mere act of utterance, it is also true that words must be wedded to intelligence for the full force of prayer to become manifest. After all, that is what the old penny catechism meant when it insisted that prayer involves the "raising" of both the heart and the *mind* to God. When the "heart and mind" is raised to God the gulf between contemplation and liturgy evaporates.

The reflective component of prayer (what are these words and why am I saying them?) also helps us to identify those prayer formulations which have taken on the status of a classic. In that category, the Lord's Prayer is preeminent not only because it comes from the Lord but also because in the tradition its meaning has never been fully plumbed. That is evident both because of the long tradition of commentary on it and because it is a prayer which the great figures of prayer turn to with such evident ease. Beyond that, every age must rediscover it precisely as "their" prayer. It is for this reason that an early monastic writer like Cassian could see the prayer as being paradigmatic for the ascetic monk, while contemporary writers like Leonardo Boff and David Crosby could write a book on saying the Lord's Prayer as subversive activity and link it with Latin American liberation theology.

While working on this chapter I asked a number of persons if they could contribute a classic prayer to my repertoire. The sample I worked with was both random and unscientific. The suggestions ran the gamut from liturgical prayers ("I love belting out the *Gloria*," one friend said) to prayers that trigger deep emotional moments of the past. The one prayer that was mentioned quite frequently was the Prayer of Saint Francis ("Lord, make me an instrument of your peace/where there is hatred, let me sow love," etc.).

The Prayer of Saint Francis. Curious. It always comes as a shock to people to learn that Saint Francis is not the author of this prayer. We do not know who wrote it, but it evidently was composed in the 1930s in Germany and slowly became reproduced and translated into the various languages of the world. I have heard it recited at many non-Roman Catholic gatherings, seen it on innumerable holy cards and plaques and calendars. It has been set to music and is regularly sung at the liturgy of our local parish.

The words of that prayer, like the words of all great prayers, combine direct discourse ("Lord") with a succinct statement of human needs and human failures. It is, at the same time, praise and confession, petition and thanksgiving—those four basic energizers of prayer. Its words are simple and set in those antitheses that so well articulate the distance between "what is" and "what should be."

All classic prayers express not only the sentiments of the writer or speaker of the prayer (how Franciscan the Prayer of Francis seems!) but also take on a generality with which others can identify. That identification occurs either because the sentiments are my sentiments or the words of the prayer align me with a tradition of praise with which I have deep sympathy. In the latter case, for example, I find it very hard to describe either to myself or others the power that comes from hearing the Hail Mary recited. It is beyond nostalgia; it speaks to my past as a Catholic and the vague sense that somehow those centuries of praise for the Virgin are part of the Catholic tradition.

And the prayer words of the Catholic of the future? Who can answer that question except to say that some prayers will always remain in the tradition because they define it and give it continuity and provide it with a sense of union through time and space. What would cause us (or who would desire) to abandon the eucharistic canon which has been at the heart of the Roman liturgy since the late second century? Who could conceive of a Catholic Christian bereft of the Lord's Prayer or the Ave Maria or the sign of the cross? Who would think of scrapping the classic formulations of the eucharistic canon or those chaste collects of the Lenten liturgy?

Furthermore, prayers remain the same because their words in all their simplicity transcend the moment. Will the believer of the future not be able to say, like Isaiah, "Here am I. Send me"? Will the conditions of life change so much that the future believer will find the words of the psalmist irrelevant? Will we not need to cry out "Though I am sometimes afraid, yet put I my trust in thee"? Will we not be able to cry out, as did Jesus using the words of the psalmist, "Into thy hands I commend my spirit"? Phrases and prayers like this transcend words or formula precisely because they bear behind them accumulated meanings that simply cannot be detached from the words themselves.

Yet, at the same time, certain words and phrases erode or demand abandonment. New words come into being; new formulations are required. Like the psalmist, we also will have to learn to "sing a new song." That is why we must encourage people to reformulate prayers. Those who look with horror (or, worse, condescending amusement) at the new feminist prayers and/or liturgies fail to see what is going on. The very fact that language is being reinvented tells us words must be rediscovered, relearned, and resaid in order for religious address to come into a freshness of being. That need explains why, in a similar way, the greatest of our theologians have always been interested in the composition of prayers. I have in mind not only a contemporary figure like Karl Rahner who has given us a river of prayers, meditations, and new creedal formulations but also that tradition which runs back to Newman in the last century, Thomas Aquinas in the Middle Ages, Augustine in the patristic period, to the writers of the New Testament church itself. After all, did not John, the most theological of the evangelists, begin his great Gospel with a hymn of praise, appropriately enough, to the Word who was made flesh? And was he not borrowing from the Book of Genesis when he wrote that hymn?

A Prayer

Altus prosator, vetustus
Dierum et ingenitus
Erat absque origine primordii et crepidine,
Est et erit in saecula
saeculorum infinitus.

Great Begetter, ancient of days and unborn
You were before the beginning of time and space
Infinite you are and will be
World without end. Amen

My choice of this prayer, written by Saint Columba of Iona in the sixth century, may seem a curious one. It is at the least a very personal choice, but it can be justified on the grounds that the early Irish Christians were drunk on the mystery of God in Christ and the power of language. Columba himself (521–597), according to an old hagiographical tradition, defended poets at the Irish court against the charge that they were too self-important. He was proud to be numbered among their ranks.

Columba, like many of the Irish poets—most of them anonymous—gave us aphoristic prayers, written either in Gaelic or Latin, that are characterized by an economy of language, a striking capacity for the apt image (they used nature in their spirituality centuries before Francis), and a deep passion for the reality of Christ. Some of those prayers, like the "Breastplate of Saint Patrick" (Christ with me/Christ before me/Christ behind me, etc.), written in Gaelic by an anonymous eighth-century monk, have remained popular to this day. It would be very difficult for anyone impressed with the Franciscan spirit not to be moved by the poem-prayer of another eighth-century monk who writes (in the translation of Brendan Kennelly): "Only a fool would fail/To praise God in his might/When the tiny mindless birds/Praise him in their flight."

It is in the words of those poet/ascetics that the conjunction of deep faith, powerful language, and an absence of artifice come together into a coherent whole. Those fragments, a millennium in distance from us, are authentic tokens of the intimate tie of the power of language and the deep springs of faith. They are poetic creations in the deepest meaning of the word *poetic*.

Some of these early prayers and poems may be found in *Treasury of Irish Religious Verse*, edited by Patrick Murray (New York: Crossroad, 1986).

A Note on Readings

The relationship between poetry and prayer has engaged the attention of many scholars and writers in this century. A good survey and critique of these theories may be found in William Noon's *Poetry and Prayer* (New Brunswick, NJ: Rutgers University Press, 1967). Nathan Scott's *The Wild Prayer of Longing* (New Haven, CT: Yale University Press, 1971) is an excellent example of applied criticism in this area. Karl Rahner's essay "Priest and Poet" can be found in *Theological Investigations* 3 (Baltimore: Helicon, 1967).

Some ideas on the Lord's Prayer that appear in this chapter were written in a different manner in my article "We Dare to Say 'Our Father,' " *Commonweal* (May 8, 1987), pp. 291–92. The classic work on the Lord's Prayer in the New Testament is still Joachim Jeremias's *The Prayers of Jesus* (Philadelphia: Fortress, 1978). There is an enormous range of material on the prayer to be found in *The Lord's Prayer and Jewish Liturgy*, edited by Jakob Petuchowski and Michael Brocke (London: Burns and Oates, 1978). Jean Carmignac's *Recherches sur le Notre Père* (Paris: Letouzey, 1969) provides an abundant survey of patristic and medieval commentary. See, among others, Leonard Boff's *The Lord's Prayer* (Maryknoll, NY: Orbis, 1982) and Michael Crosby's *Thy Will Be Done: The Our Father as Subversive Activity* (Maryknoll, NY: Orbis, 1977)—studies of the prayer from the perspective of liberation theology. My citation of Maximus comes from his "Commentary on the Lord's Prayer" in *Maximus Confessor: Se-*

lected Writings, translated by George Berthold (Mahwah, NJ: Paulist, 1985), pp. 99–126. For a rather Thomistic reading of the Lord's Prayer Raissa Maritain's *Notes on the Lord's Prayer* (New York: P. J. Kenedy, 1964), a book edited and finished by Jacques Maritain, is still useful. Gordon Bahr, "The Use of the Lord's Prayer in the Primitive Church," *Journal of Biblical Literature* 84 (1965), pp. 153–59, has an interesting discussion of the patristic notion of the prayer as an "outline."

For a full but not exhaustive list of studies, see Monica Dorneisch, editor, *Vater Unser—Bibliographie* (Freiburg im Breisgau: Oratio Dominica, 1982).

Collections of prayers that have "classic" status still appear with regularity; two recent ones are: *The Oxford Book of Prayer,* edited by George Appleton (New York: Oxford University Press, 1985), and *The New Book of Christian Prayers,* edited by Tony Castle (New York: Crossroad, 1986). There is a generous selection of early Irish prayers and poems in the *Treasury of Irish Religious Verse,* edited by Patrick Murray (New York: Crossroad, 1986).

3

GESTURES

The greatest utility of bodies is
in their use as signs. For from them are
made many signs necessary for our salvation.

Guigo the Carthusian

For the past few years an unknown person has been sending me envelopes full of clippings, photocopies, manifestos, pamphlets, etc., representing what can only be called the far Right wing of Roman Catholicism. There are philippics against liberal theologians, testimonies about the Blessed Virgin's appearances in Yugoslavia and Bayside, New York, keening laments about the social and moral degradation of Roman Catholicism globally and the North American Church in particular. It is not clear to me whether my unnamed benefactor sees me as a kindred soul or as one who might be saved before it is too late. I suppose most people would jettison the material with all due speed but, I must confess, I find it rather fascinating and generally read every word of it. At times, the material is downright interesting. Recently, an essay came my way (published I know not where; I have only the photocopy before me) by one Michael Davies who, judging by his biography, is not unsympathetic to the decidedly unsympathetic Archbishop Marcel Lefebvre.

The essay argues that the liturgical changes since the Vatican II reforms—the turning of the altar toward the people, the disappearance of the traditional usages connected with chalice and ciborium, the increased emphasis on standing, Com-

49

munion in the hand, etc.—are profound indications that the
"reforms" are, in fact, a diabolical turn of affairs in which the
majesty of God is insulted and the mystery of the real presence of Christ in the Eucharist is denigrated. The author
quotes a German Catholic woman who sees standing at Mass
during the canon as a triumph of Nazi ideology, citing the
Nazi slogan that a "German does not kneel before his God; a
German stands before his God" (*Ein Deutscher kniet nicht
vor seinen Herrgott, ein Deutscher steht vor seinen Gott*) and
Doctor Goebbels's belief that the Catholic church was a
"Jewish corruption" that reduced Germans to the status of
slaves on their knees.

My purpose in mentioning this tendentious essay is not to
dignify but to underscore a rather important point that it
makes, however unwittingly: that prayer in its manifold
forms can be understood (or better, must be understood) in
terms of the gestures that accompany it. Prayer as speech is
almost inevitably accompanied by prayer as gesture. Furthermore, these gestures, whether social or individual, give us
deep insight into the nature and character of prayer if we simply avert to the significance of those gestures and attempt to
decode them. Thus, the author of the pamphlet mentioned
above sees the increased amount of standing at the liturgy as
a powerful indication of radical dis-ease in the contemporary
church. The abandonment of kneeling is viewed as a visual
proof that the old sense of the Transcendent has slipped away
to be replaced by something not quite sacred.

The author of that diatribe is not well informed (some early
Fathers forbade kneeling in church precisely because Christians were not to imitate slave behavior) but makes a point:
Gestures in worship and prayer have a profound significance.
"Reading" such gestures can tell us a great deal about theology, piety, social attitudes, and so on. It was not uncommon
for earlier spiritual writers to understand the symbolic gestures of the body as signs of the interior disposition of the
soul. The author is also correct, one hastens to add, that the
shift from kneeling to standing most likely does "say" something of religious significance. At this point we might wish,

however, to stay at a more theoretical level in our consideration of bodily gestures.

A brief but very general example might make the point with economy. One of the celebrated distinctions in the field of religion is between religions that emphasize immanence and those that affirm transcendence. The distinction is an important one but hard to grasp at a certain level since a religious tradition can manifest elements of both. Thus, the Bible affirms, at different places and in different ways, that God is absolutely transcendent in that divinity is over and above the world of nature and history but, likewise, God is immanent in the processes of history and, preeminently, in the Incarnation. It has been a perennial task in theology to do full justice to both of those notions when discussing the Christian concept of God.

When dealing with the raw distinction of transcendence and immanence as a concept, I often tell my students that one easy way to understand the distinction between the two is to focus not on a definition but on an image. Think of the Moslem world when it is called to prayer. Everyone has seen newsreel footage of Muslims on their prayer rugs (in the mountains of Afghanistan or in the square of a principal mosque in Saudi Arabia) kneeling with their heads bowed down to the ground. This is the position of submission (Islam means submission) and represents, graphically, that Allah is one, transcendent, and worthy of total and unabashed adoration. Contrast that image with the most common depiction of the Buddha. The Buddha (the word means enlightened one; it is a title, not a personal name) sits cross-legged, hands folded, eyes nearly shut, with the head held either directly forward or slightly downcast. The Buddha is not depicted with a vertical gesture (pointed to the heavens) nor in a state of abasement. The Buddha finds truth within. The Muslim gestures with the self as a pole opposite to the transcendent power of God. The Buddha learns that there is no self by turning inward on a voyage of pure discovery. There is no polar opposite because enlightenment consists of learning that there is no polarity. In those two stylized gestures the distinction between a religion of transcendence and a religion of immanence is patent.

A close look at gestures in the Roman Catholic tradition tells us not only about the nature of prayer but also about the complexity of our attitudes toward prayer. This struck me when, at the Sunday liturgy some weeks ago, I happened to watch the gestures of people during the singing of the Lord's Prayer. Standing (why, by the bye, do we stand to say that prayer at the liturgy after kneeling through the eucharistic prayer?) as a congregation I noticed that some families or couples joined hands for the prayer while others (charismatics?) extended their hands like the priest, while still others joined their hands in the traditional gesture of supplicatory prayer. What struck me as a kind of visual lesson was a complex manifestation of prayer that was communal and private, public and linked to various forms of devotionalism, with elements of both transcendence (the arms extended and raised) and immanent (the joining of hands). Furthermore, what was occurring had the sanction of community acceptance. Everyone observed the basic ground rules (nobody, for example, sat through the prayer) and nobody used gestures that were in dissonance with what was expected of worshiping Catholics; nobody, for example, sang the Lord's Prayer while standing on one hand. Finally, however unobstrusively, the gestures also spoke to the rest of the congregation saying, by turns, "I am a charismatic" or "We have been to Marriage Encounter" or "I am devout." The gestures of the congregation, in short, had a dual significance: They spoke of an attitude toward God and made a statement about the social understanding of those assuming various kinds of bodily gestures.

We should also note how primordial some of those gestures are. The common habit of extending the arms (e.g., the gesture of the priest when praying the Lord's Prayer) is an ancient one. In many Semitic languages the verb meaning "to raise the arms" can also mean, in context, "to pray." It was a gesture also known to Greek and Roman culture and was taken over in Christianity as the "Orans" figure in early Christian art (it is frequently seen in catacomb frescos); it exists, as we have noted, to this day. The Orans gesture of praying with extended hands while standing is amply attested in the texts of the ancient churches. Here are some typical expressions from early Syriac spiritual literature:

> What then is prayer? And what is petition? And why do we stand in prayer facing the East? (Anonymous—sixth century)

> At such a time [i.e., of prayer] it is appropriate that we stand with wakeful and attentive mind combined with a sense of awe and trembling. (Martyrius—sixth century)

> Someone who shows a reverential posture during prayer, by stretching out his hands to heaven as he stands modestly, or by falling on his face to the ground, will be accounted worthy. (Isaac of Nineveh—seventh century)

There is a further point. The various individual attitudes expressed by gesture were in the context of the common gesture of (a) being at the liturgy as a community and (b) acquiescing in the common custom of standing demanded by the rules of liturgical courtesy and decorum. In other words, as we will insistently note in these pages, there is both a multiplicity and unity held in tension by the right(s) of spiritual freedom and the constraints of the communal tradition of the believing community. Even in the Syriac tradition cited above, there is advice about kneeling as an act of penance or penitence; of sitting with the eyes fixed on the chest (i.e., the heart) in meditation; of prostrating oneself repeatedly in adoration, etc. These are all practices common in both the Eastern and Western churches today.

It is interesting to note that the Gospels give us rather fragmentary but crucial information about gesture and posture in prayer. The first, and most obvious, thing we learn is that Jesus insists that there be a harmony between prayer and the manner in which prayer is expressed: "And when you pray, you must not be like the hypocrites: for they love to stand and pray in the synagogues and at the street corners, that they may be seen by men"; and conversely: "When you pray, go into your room and shut the door and pray to your Father who is in secret . . . " (Matt. 6:5–6a). The obvious point is that gestures/postures in prayer are either in harmony with or in contrast to one's desire to relate to God. Hence, Jesus resisted the temptation to fall down and worship Satan precisely because the primal relationship was not to Satan but to the Father who alone is to be worshiped (see Matt. 4:9–10). As the passion of Jesus begins to unfold he, in fact, did "fall to the ground" (Mark 14:35) or "fell on his face" (Matt. 26:39) or, more prosaically, "knelt down" (Luke 22:41) in the Garden of Gethsemane.

All of the examples we have cited above are examples of "body language." To pray pharisaically is not to pray at all; it is to posture. To "fall down and worship" Satan would be to enact a gesture of adoration. By contrast, the "falling on the face" in the Garden of Gethsemane is precisely an act of religious submission. Those gestures in the New Testament are, in short, hieratic conventions that indicate in precise places the relationship of the pray-er to God. Such gestures, to be sure, are not peculiar to the New Testament. They have a history behind them in the narrative. They should not be looked on necessarily as models for prayer since they function as conventions in the biblical narrative as well.

Nonetheless, those gestures found in the Bible carry with them a good deal of theological meaning. Thus, we are meant to see something imitable in the publican who stands inconspicuously in the temple beating his breast with his eyes cast down (see Luke 18:9–14) just as we are to praise the sick woman who had faith enough to touch only the hem of his garment (see Mark 5:28; Luke 8:44). In both of those scenes it is position/location/bodily attitude that gives depth and pungency to the depth of the pray-ers' faith. It is prayer by corporeal gesture.

In fact, when one looks at the body language of prayer in the Christian tradition, what one sees is that certain gestures and postures develop connaturally in the history of spirituality and others develop in tandem with the development of specific spiritualities and devotions. Leaving aside the more formulaic gestures demanded by liturgical prayer (to be discussed below), one can say that the body language of prayer is as varied as the impulses of prayer itself.

Liturgical scholars like Paul Bradshaw have shown that the early church reflected at times on the appropriate gestures of prayer. Origen, for example, argues that the best manner of prayer is with head uncovered and hands upraised, although he notes that circumstances may be such that a person has to pray sitting or even (in the case of illness) lying down. When traveling or at business, he notes, it might even be necessary to pray while pretending not to pray. As early as the time of Tertullian there are instructions about how to pray and encouragement to initiate prayers with a gesture that we now call the sign of the cross. A close reading of these early writers indicates that they were keenly interested in the larger gestures of prayer: appropriate times both for the assembly and at home, the times of fasting and prayer, the character of the social groupings, etc. These formal considerations would, in time, develop into that complex ceremonial law of liturgy which we call *rubrics* and take on a quasi-normative character.

The development of formal gestures in the liturgy was accompanied by a slow development of gestures that should accompany private devotions and those paraliturgical devotions that emerged in patristic and monastic circles and which were eventually found full blown in the devotionalism of the medieval period.

This becomes clear from a quick consideration of a pseudonymous booklet published in Bologna around 1260 entitled *The Nine Ways of Prayer of Saint Dominic*. Put together after the saint's death (1221), the author noted that many treatises had been written on prayer but none speaks of the way in which the "soul uses the members of the body." The booklet then goes on to describe the range of these gestures, from bowing humbly before the altar and repeated prostrations before a crucifix to standing with arms raised directly above the head or sitting in the quiet of the cell meditating on the pages of sacred scripture or while walking from one destination to another. Some of these gestures were described as being in imitation of biblical usages or as reflections of Christ's postures (extending the arms in prayer after the manner of Christ on the cross—a usage as old as the third century, when Tertullian gives it that precise meaning)—or, more simply, as illustrating that one could pray under any and all circumstances. In sum, we can say that the motive behind the writing of the *Nine Ways* is not dissimilar to an observation made by Saint Thomas Aquinas in the *Summa* (II IIae q. 84 a. 2) that adoration should involve the body as well as the soul because every person is a composite creature who owes adoration with his or her whole being.

The *Nine Ways* has behind it a millennium of usages, customs, and prescriptions for prayer. If we look forward to our own day we see that the situation has not changed but the emphases have. For example, one sees less today an emphasis on prayer-gestures that directly mimic, say, the passion gestures of Christ. Rarely, outside of Mediterranean usage, does one find extravagant imitations of the Crucified One once so common as an ascetical practice in the religious orders or as practices of private devotions observable in many older parishes or shrine churches. In fact, many fastidious believers find something primitive, threatening, or even degrading about such body language, as an observation of Anglo tourist/pilgrims on the behavior of the Mestizo peasants at a shrine like that of Our Lady of Guadalupe attests.

The decline of such formal devotionalism (think of the once popular practice of the stations of the cross done with a mixture of walking, pausing, genuflecting, kneeling, and standing) does not mean a decline in the life of private and/or nonliturgical prayer. On the contrary. One of the conspicuous signs of post-Vatican II vitality has been an increased appetite for the spiritual life. If one were to generalize about that interest it would not be wrong to note its emphasis on the kinds of prayer most appropriately called meditative or contemplative. There has been an authentic search for the older forms of prayer and meditation and a veritable explosion of resources ranging from retreats/workshops to the publication of the old spiritual classics to aid those who wish to pray in this manner. There is, further, a whole range of new gestures that have developed as prayer and social action have become combined. That is clear from a consideration of everything from pro-life pilgrimages to antimilitarism protests. Recent books on prayer have emphasized the need for silence both interior and exterior and the need to seem "comfortable" in prayer.

The requirement that a context of silence is necessary for prayer is hardly peculiar to the contemporary scene. It is the motive for founding monasteries in out-of-the-way places and a commonplace in all ascetical literature. The contemporary emphasis on silence is centered on the deep conviction that, to an unparalleled degree, we are bombarded with outside stimuli that has the power to alienate us from ourselves and, ultimately, from God. The search for that silence means not only a quiet place but a quiet mind free from the sensory echoes of the world and the distractions of everyday concerns. We need to be listeners but, paradoxically enough, we need to listen for silence. It could be argued, it seems to me, that the basis of all of Thomas Merton's spirituality (and, further, a fundamental reason for his enormous popularity) is this search for exterior and interior silence.

One component of that silence, these modern writers on prayer insist, is to be at home with the body at least to the extent that bodily discomfort not become an obstacle in the search for the quiet of silence. Hence the common advice that one pray/meditate in a comfortable chair or in some position that does not distract from the business at hand. Thus, Thomas Keating describes a contemplative prayer group's session as consisting of a slow contemplative period of walking, a period or periods of sitting, and a concluding communal prayer. Behind those gestures is a desire to provide the body with recollected silence rather than to "forget" the body.

This contemporary emphasis on what I will simply call the "gestures of comfort" has behind it a theological insight that is worth bringing to the fore. The honorably old description of prayer as raising the "heart and mind and soul" to God had the undesired but inevitable result of making prayer into a "spiritual" or, worse, "intellectual" activity. That resulted (or could result) in driving a wedge between the body and soul of a person. One of the great aims of the current writers on prayer is to convince people that a more holistic approach is needed if prayer is to be a component of the contemporary experience. The contemporary masters/mistresses of the prayer life would, in effect, redefine prayer as the "lifting up of the *person* to God." They see this as a reappropriation of the ancient tradition of contemplative prayer and an attack on the notion, common since the early Renaissance, that prayer is primarily an intellectual exercise oriented toward God as object.

This emphasis on the notion of prayer as the relationship of the whole person to God is part of the larger attempt to recover the idea that we are an incarnate people and not spirits somehow captured in bodies with the spirit(s) being the fit nexus between us and God. If, for example, older ascetical practices have fallen into disfavor (most of us would fast for the good of the waistline but few for the triggering of the Kingdom), it is not simply because this generation of believers is less tough than those who came before us but because the modern sensibility refuses to see the body as an implacably recalcitrant instrument that needs to be brought to heel. That may or may not be a correct judgment but it seems to be a given in our world.

This is not to deny that we, unlike our forebearers, are less in need of personal discipline or that asceticism is fit only for the dustbin of history. It is, rather, that we need to reconceptualize discipline and ascesis in terms of our self-understanding of who we are and how we stand in the world. Meister Eckhart, hardly a sybarite, once remarked that it is far easier to remain alone in a desert than in a crowd. Circumstance, in short, is everything.

Scholars like Margaret Miles have not only underscored the persistence of asceticism as a constitutive part of Christian spirituality but have also attempted to cleanse it of aberrations (those, for example, which derive from a kind of angelism). Miles, for instance, argues that asceticism has as its goal the cleansing of "sluggishness" or "torpor" or "smallness of soul"—conditions that the early spiritual fathers and mothers call *accedia*. Understood from that angle, asceticism helps us overcome those conditions—ranging from compulsive sexuality to media addiction—which hold us back from that authentic sense of self-possession which the early literature refers to as purity of heart. The need to live such a life can be rendered concrete by simply imagining what incarnate temptations would assail Saint Anthony were he located not in the early desert experience but in the midst of our own suburban or urban landscape.

To this point we have reflected on those gestures that we assume, either for the moment or as a style of life, through individual choice. We need to underscore, however, that prayer is never exclusively individual. Prayer is also—and equally—a social phenomenon. When we speak of prayer we must speak of corporate or social prayer. We must speak, in short, of the liturgy.

We begin by noting that the very fact that one chooses to worship in community constitutes in itself the most important primary gesture of prayer. That becomes clear when we ask the question: What does it mean to go to church ("going to church" being our shorthand phrase for public worship)? It means a goodly number of things.

In the very first place, the act (gesture) of going to worship in common affirms, in its very structure, the willingness of the person to join his or her self to a larger social reality. The gesture of going stands as a radical (but not antithetical) alternative to prayer behind closed doors in the privacy of one's own space.

That gesture of choosing to pray as a social group seems unworthy of comment since it appears to be such a commonplace. Its profound significance becomes a bit more clear, however, when we realize how people quite frequently make that gesture not as an act of habit but to say something of primordial importance. In the rather fluid days of this postconciliar church examples of such message-laden gestures are not hard to come by. Some people, for instance, stop going to church not because they "get out of the habit" but as a means of "voting with their feet." Others choose alternatives to make a theological statement. In my home town, for example, there is a monthly Mass (held at a local Holiday Inn) celebrated by an itinerant priest who uses the Tridentine rite and fiddleback chasubles. Those who attend are doing so to satisfy their spiritual yearnings and to make a public statement about their disdain for the "modernist" new liturgy of Rome.

From the other side of the spectrum some women are gathering together for feminist celebrations of worship. Both of these are examples of marginal groups, to be sure, but they do reflect the intuitive understanding that people have of such public gestures. Those gestures have within them both a social component and an expression of spiritual need.

For the vast majority of those who go to Mass on a regular basis there is a thick cluster of messages embedded in their gesture of participation, which are equally social and theological.

There is the open sign of belonging to a particular community; the act of participating in the liturgy says, in that act, that one is a Catholic. A "nonpracticing" Catholic, after all, is understood as one who does not go to church and/or participate in the sacramental life of the church. To go to Mass is to say that one is a Catholic and, at a deeper level, a sharer in the common life of those who so identify themselves in time and space: "Father, hear the prayers of the family you have gathered here before you./In mercy and love unite all your children wherever they may be" (Eucharistic Prayer III).

Beyond the gesture of simply choosing to go to Mass are those body-language expressions by which we orchestrate our behavior at the liturgy itself. Some years ago Monsignor Ronald Knox likened that behavior to a stately dance and invited us to watch the Mass in "slow motion." Even at a sociological level it is an interesting exercise. Many people kneel at their place before Mass begins to pray privately and, one guesses, to re-collect themselves—to put themselves in the mood of receptivity. As the liturgy begins there is a nearly unconscious response of standing and sitting. It always amuses me to watch people sit after the reading of the Gospel with an air of resignation, which seems to say to the priest shuffling his notes for the coming homily "Please try and keep my attention; please say something that will make me sit bolt upright!"

The practice of kneeling after the Sanctus (and until the great Amen, which prefaces the singing of the Lord's Prayer) is a carry-over from the old liturgy, but it is also a sign, however imperfectly understood, that the great mystery of Christ's

presence among us is—despite our casual acceptance of it—
an awe-ful event. That period of kneeling is where the focus
of communal and private devotion coalesces and the transcendent reality of God is celebrated. The gesture of kneeling
at this point in the liturgy, peculiar to Western Catholicism,
reflects a cluster of theological understandings that developed
over the long history of the Catholic tradition. It is a gesture,
borrowed from the language of human abasement and servi-
tude, that celebrates both the transcendent reality of God and
the immanent presence of God in Christ in the liturgical
mysteries. Its passing may, or may not be, a good thing but it
does most emphatically signal a different understanding of
the Eucharist in particular and worship in general.

The period of kneeling contrasts nicely with the standing
for the Lord's Prayer and the subsequent break in the rhythm
of the liturgy when we turn from the altar or pulpit to one
another to exchange a sign of peace. When that practice was
introduced into the reformed liturgy there was (and still, in
pockets, is) a fair amount of resistance and/or awkwardness in
its implementation. That awkwardness derived, I suspect,
from the Catholic taboo of speaking to others in church (parents would cuff kids who did that at Mass!) and from the
deeply held belief that the only focus for the person was toward the altar and the mysteries it represented. To turn to
others with familiar gestures just appeared *too* familiar and
too informal for an older generation of Catholics. It took time
to get people to see that such a gesture of unity and reconciliation was a profoundly satisfying prelude for the reception of
Communion. It is most edifying to see that gesture being
done today without any self-consciousness or stiffness. It is
one of the loveliest gifts the liturgical reforms have given us.

The kiss of peace was almost as big a change in traditional
Catholicism as the manner of receiving Holy Communion.
The old custom of kneeling at the altar rail with hands folded
(and, often, placed under a white cloth that covered the rail itself) while the priest placed a Communion wafer on the tongue
and an altar boy held a paten under the chin of the recipient
was gone. In the vast majority of parish liturgies the people
come and stand to take Communion in hand and to drink

from the Communion cup. In fairness to the conservative critics we must say that such a shift of posture is intimately linked with a theological shift in the understanding of the Eucharist. From the narrow focus on "Real Presence" developed largely in the early Middle Ages and refined in the controversies of the Reformation, the church has attempted to get back to the older notion of Communion as union with Christ in community until, as Paul says in his famous passage in First Corinthians, Christ "comes again" (11:26).

The eucharistic theology, worked out imperfectly at the Second Vatican Council, attempted to mitigate the purely transcendental view of the presence of Christ as *mysterium* into a more nuanced understanding of Christ truly present both under the species of bread and wine and the presence of Christ among those who celebrate those mysteries as a believing community: hence, an emphasis that was, simultaneously, transcendent (Christ as glorified among us sacramentally) and immanent (Christ dwelling amid the worshiping community). The "architectural" gesture reinforcing that new understanding can be seen in the separation of the altar of worship from the altar (tabernacle) for the reservation of the Eucharist.

There is a great paradox about attendance at the liturgy. It is something that is different—an interruption in our daily and weekly round—but it is also familiar because it so easily fits into our schedule: Monday we go to work; Friday we begin the weekend; Sunday we go to church. It is difficult not to allow the gestures at Mass (like the prayers and the readings and the homilies) settle into routine and reflex. In fact, like most religious observances in a tolerant society, the great enemy of faith is not ignorance or strangeness but familiarity. Familiarity breeds not contempt always but familiarity. That familiarity is reinforced because our gestures and our prayers are ritualized. It was Mircea Eliade who shrewdly pointed out that when ritualized gestures are evacuated of meaning one then ends up with magic, not worship.

If we think of the liturgy as the great gesture of the believing community as it recalls, represents, and reenacts the saving mysteries of Christ, then the gesture ought to "say" so

clearly and with profound conviction. Let me float a somewhat preposterous example to make my point. A too literal
liturgical adapter stationed at a Wall Street parish might be
tempted to conduct the liturgy decked out in a three-piece
suit using a briefcase for an altar and employing a glass of
white wine and a loaf of gourmet bread for the eucharistic
elements. I would say: Resist such ideas strenuously. It would
seem to me that the precise purpose of the gesture of liturgy
is to provide a counterpoint to the workaday world, not to
reinforce that world or celebrate it. The worst excesses of liturgical experimentation (think of the gruesome "clown"
Masses and the like that have been inflicted on the poor people of God) come precisely from those who see no tension between the liturgy and the world of the quotidian.

This is not to argue that the liturgy exists free from culture.
The move to Africanize or Mexicanize (or whatever) the liturgy springs from a genuine resistance to the notion that
liturgy develops by divine fiat from Western European cultural imperatives. The cultural forms may (and probably
should be) pluriform, but the total gesture which is the liturgy ought to speak as an epiphany and a sign (sacrament) of
the breakthrough of God's graciousness into our reality: "And
the Word was made flesh and dwelt among us." To so "imma-
nentize" the liturgy as to render it indistinguishable from culture is to trivialize it and, worse, render it impotent before
the inevitable erosion of the cultural moment. To marry the
spirit of the times, a wise person once said, is soon to find
oneself a widower.

The "differentness" of the liturgy helps us to enter both the
time and the space of a different reality that says, in the very
act of entrance, we are believers and witnesses to the saving
power of Jesus the Christ. Every individual and communal
gesture which makes up the complex of that great gesture is
an enfleshed act of faith, which is to say, an act of prayer. The
great task of the believer who makes that gesture is to affirm
the truth of the liturgy as it is experienced in gesture and
then to translate it into the daily round of life. The means
and the centrality of that exercise will be taken up in a separate chapter. Suffice it to say here that the intimate connec-

tion between the communal gesture of worship and the daily round of life precludes any suspicion that I am arguing for a fully otherworldly kind of religion that retreats from the world for worship. It would be more precise to say that in the liturgy we periodically pause, in a willed act of conscious gesture, to celebrate what we mean about our entire life and its final significance.

The liturgy is, of course, profoundly and irreducibly public but, in the last analysis, the public gestures of the liturgy do share with our private gestures of prayer and devotion one thing in common: They celebrate differentness—they are a break in our pace of routine. This is as true of the person who kneels at bedside before retirement as it is for the person who dresses on a Sunday morning and goes off to Mass. The gestures of prayer say—to many or to oneself—that there is an orientation/attitude in life that admits of God. When those gestures color the texture of a life they transform a life, as it were, into celebration.

It is that conjunction of gesture in daily life and at the formal moments of worship that creates a holism which we can call "Christian living." It may be too much to think that we can recreate that Catholic "atmosphere" so praised by spiritual writers of a past age: Mom and Dad and the (many) kids praying the rosary after supper along with Cardinal Cushing on the radio, but it is not unrealistic to think that the presence of the liturgy by extension through the sacramentals is hopelessly gone. It may take new strategies and new ideas, but the gestures of faith can be made pertinent to a whole range of social structures whether it be the traditional nuclear family or the now ubiquitous single-parent family. The how and why of these strategies are too varied to discuss (although we can note in passing the phenomenal success of the base community as a social gesture created to fill real religious and social needs), but their utility and their need is beyond discussion.

The power of simple gestures, developed for specific needs and social settings, that extend the great gestures of the liturgy into the familiar and familial depends to a large extent on how willingly theologians work to recover a sense of the ordinary religious gestures of our Catholic culture. It is, in my estimation, a sad turn of events that so much contemporary spirituality, both in practice and in theory, appeals to a limited elite who have time or resources to have a "contemplative experience" at some converted dude ranch in the West. What does the harried parent or working person make of the advice, given in all seriousness by one noted American spirituality guru, that one could respond to the visionary writings of Hildegard of Bingen by a personal reaction consisting of doing pottery or writing poetry or composing songs? There is a kind of New Age psychobabble that infects "spirituality" to an alarming degree in some quarters.

It would seem to me that we would be better advised to try and recapture the extraordinary in the ordinary, primordial gestures of our prayer life. There are many of them, many burnished by custom and others lying in neglect that beg for a hermeneutics of retrieval.

My plea would be to reflect on the power of people saying grace before meals, to cite a common example. In that act, so common as to be banal, there is a reservoir of solid theology that merely demands a teasing-out into explicit terminology. Let me use that example and ask about the significance of a group of people joining hands and "giving thanks." I ask the following questions:

- Why join hands? Why bow heads? (Are we affirming both the immanence of God with us and our equal recognition that God is beyond us?)
- Why is *thanksgiving* so natural at this moment and how is it connected to adoration? (Have we ever, for example, thought about how truly bountiful our bounty is?)
- When we join hands we do it as a sign of reconciliation and of family or friendship. How far is that circle of friendship/family to be extended? (It would be hardly appropriate to do so at table, but might it not be worthwhile sometime to reflect on who it is we would not join hands with? How far away from our primary relationships do we have to go before we reach that person? And what should we do about it?)
- What about those who have no clear reason or resources about which they can be thankful for? (If we thank God for our

bounty and are indifferent to those who do not share in it we are, at best, smug and, at worst, at odds with what we are supposed to be all about.)

Let me not hammer too insistently on this business of grace before meals. The whole subject came to me clearly one afternoon when I was taking my turn at our local Saint Vincent de Paul soup kitchen. Our custom is to say the Lord's Prayer before eating because most of our guests either find the "Catholic" grace too preemptory or do not know the words. Who can judge, but God, what goes on in the hearts of those who pray there each day before they eat? Some pray with intensity, some as the price of eating, some out of respect. But one thing is very clear: They do not pray as a community; indeed, they are the antitype of community. They are isolated in their bewilderment or in the haze of alcohol or the tortures of schizophrenic voices or in the defeat of a life that has simply beat them. Their only community is in the bonds of their common role as the marginal ones who touch, ever so lightly, our sense of community.

What is also clear—at least to me—is that I pray with them not as a member of a community of brothers and sisters. I am too middle class, too timid, too cerebral, and too selfish really to say that they are one with me. I even pray at Mass, in a rote fashion, that we may all be one, but the unvarnished truth is that the prospect that such a prayer would be answered strikes me with terror. I make the first gestures of prayer and pathetic gestures of help, but I do not want to see through the full implications of what my mouth says or my body symbolizes. Only saints do that.

What I have noted about something as common as grace before meals could be found in almost all of the gestures of the faith, from making the sign of the cross to the elaborate choreography of the liturgy. What is at base, however, is the irreducible fact that gestures in their fullness are a language, a language which, when fully decoded, is so radically demanding that we find it safer, for the most part, to keep it at a safe and unreflective distance.

A Prayer

I extended my hands
And hallowed my Lord.

For the extension of my hands
is his sign.

And my extension
is the upright cross.

Hallelujah.

This short hymn, reproduced in its entirety, is Ode 27 of the *Odes of Solomon*. The *Odes of Solomon* is Christianity's earliest hymn book dating, perhaps, to the late first century. The hymns may well have had a baptismal setting and come from the ancient church of Syriac-speaking Christians.

As this hymn makes clear, the position of standing at prayer is in imitation of Christ on the cross; it is "his sign." In fact, Ode 42 begins with a nearly exact repetition of these words followed by a response of Christ who hymns his own triumph over the cross so that, in the power of his resurrection, he places his "name upon their head/because they are free and they are mine."

These early hymns, wonderful in their language and powerful in their poetry, are available in a bilingual edition: *The Odes of Solomon*, edited and translated by James H. Charlesworth (Chico, CA: Scholars Press, 1977). This volume is a corrected reprint of an edition first published by the Clarendon Press of Oxford University in 1973.

A Note on Readings

My citations of the Syriac Fathers are taken from *The Syriac Fathers on Prayer and the Spiritual Life*, introduced and translated by Sebastian Brock (Kalamazoo, MI: Cistercian Publications, 1987). The "Nine Ways of Prayer" can be found in *Early Dominicans: Selected Writings*, edited with an introduction by Simon Tugwell, O.P. (Mahwah, NJ: Paulist, 1982), pp. 94–103.

Paul F. Bradshaw's *Daily Prayer in the Early Church* (New York: Oxford University Press, 1982) has many good pages on gestures in the public prayer of the church. Thomas Keating's *Open Mind, Open Heart* (Warwick, NY: Amity House, 1986) has good observations on the relationship of gestures/postures to contemplative prayer.

Margaret Miles's *Fullness of Life: Historical Foundations for a New Asceticism* (Philadelphia: Westminster, 1981) both describes asceticism historically and argues for its pertinence today.

I have tried to think through the changes in the liturgy and how they impact on Catholic prayer life in "Sacred Space and Sacred Time: Reflections on Contemporary Catholicism," in *The Incarnate Imagination: Essays in Honor of Andrew Greeley*, edited by Ingrid Shafer (Bowling Green, OH: Bowling Green State University Popular Press, 1988), pp. 248–55.

Theological reflections on bodiliness have been summarized in Paul Philibert, "Tacit Prophecy: Some Considerations of Bodiliness," *Spirituality Today* 32 (1980), pp. 57–68. Also, see Carl E. and LaVonne Braaten, *The Living Temple: A Practical Theology of the Body and the Foods of the Earth* (New York: Harper and Row, 1976), and Charles Davis, *The Body as Spirit: The Nature of Religious Feeling* (New York: Seabury, 1976).

4

READING

Learn the Heart of God in the Word of God.

St. Gregory the Great

By reading we mean, preeminently, reading the Bible and, further, reading the Bible as an act of prayer. Reading the Bible as an act of prayer does not mean, at base, a devotional reading by which one encounters the page(s) of the scriptures and then, moved by the Spirit, prayer arises. That, surely, is a way to pray, but it is a good deal more complicated than that. In fact, the relationship of the scriptures to the prayer life of the believer is so complex that when one begins to think about it the permutations become so tangled as to create bewilderment.

If we assume, and the Catholic church has so assumed from its beginnings, that the New Testament is a product of the church and not vice versa, then we see that the scriptures themselves do not lead to prayer but are a product of it. By that I mean that the scriptures came to us as a reactive development of the earliest believers who testified to their faith in Jesus as the Christ. The Gospels were written for believers by believers. In that sense they stand as witnesses to faith and, as we have earlier argued, in their statements of faith they are also statements of prayer broadly conceived. Thus, when the Apostle John writes that the book of signs which he had written was put down on paper so that "you may believe that Jesus is the Christ, the Son of God, and that believing you

69

may have life everlasting" (20:31), the apostle is not only writing a justification for his Gospel but is also uttering a prayer of intercession for those who encounter his witness. That same sense is found quite often in Paul who, typically, calls down blessings on those who read his letters and, as in Romans and elsewhere, ends with a doxological prayer. Paul's letters, in short, are framed in prayer: "Grace to you and peace from God our Father and the Lord Jesus Christ," begins the first letter to the church at Corinth and, recalling those words, Paul ends the epistle: "The grace of the Lord Jesus be with you. My love be with you all in Christ Jesus. Amen." Variations on that prayer/blessing occur in each of the letters that Paul wrote.

Yet the matter does not rest there. The scriptures come out of a witnessing and praying community. The community, in turn, looks to those same writings both to justify the life of prayer (the early Christian writers never tire of calling up the great paradigmatic figures from the Bible who were steadfast in worship) and to use the same scriptures as their source for prayer, either by using it directly (e.g., in the recitation of the Psalms) or by borrowing its vocabulary to develop its liturgical and devotional formulae. The prayer of the church responds to and makes use of the scriptures. That relationship is caught nicely in a phrase of Saint Ambrose that the Second Vatican Council cites with approbation: "We speak to Him when we pray; we hear Him when we read the divine sayings" (see *Dogmatic Constitution on Sacred Revelation*, art. 25).

This is not to deny that the Bible is the resource for proclamation and catechesis. It most assuredly is. It is to argue that in the daily life of the church the Bible is most frequently put forward as the source of the continuing witness to the reality of Christ as it celebrates his presence in its unceasing acts of worship. At that level, at least, the Bible cannot be easily separated from worship precisely because it is read in a setting of worship and praise.

We can say, then, that the Bible is at the very core of the prayer life of the church. That position of the Bible in the life of the church is the correct way to think of the Bible in the Catholic Christian tradition. The Bible does not stand "out there" as a printed artifact; it is the continuing witness of the church's faith and worship and the wellspring of the continuation of that faithful witness to the reality of God in Jesus Christ.

The presence of the sacred scriptures in the prayer life of the church is so ubiquitous (think of the snatches of scripture in the common prayers of the rosary from the Lord's Prayer and the Hail Mary to the Glory Be to the Father and even the Creed) that most of us have absorbed a great swath of the Bible by osmosis without ever averting to its source, its context, or its full significance. The current movement to encourage regular Bible reading and Bible study, thanks to a revival initiated mainly in this century, is a partial remedy to the unreflective presence of the Bible among us, but it is not always clear to the participants in such activities what the aim of these exercises is: To confound text-quoting fundamentalists? To learn "more about" the Bible? To increase devotion? To strengthen faith? All of the above? None of the above?

The confusions of a study group mirror, to a certain degree, the manifold uses to which the Bible is put in the life of the church: It is the object of study for the theologian and exegete; it is a manual of prayer for the religious; it is a source of inspiration for the preacher; and so on. While, at a theoretical level, these partial aims form a whole, the nature of that whole is not always fully appreciated. There is a vast difference between the presuppositions of the liturgy with its broad typological reading of the entire Bible and the painstaking work of the exegete, just as there is a gulf between the preacher who tends to moralize on a given text and the monk or nun who ranges in prayer through the psalter on a regular basis. There is the further problem of "seeing" how something as formal as reading can be understood as what is assumed to be the more spontaneous act of praying.

For the person in the pew the problems are different (if for no other reason than that they have not invested the Bible with as close a look as has the exegete or theologian) but very real. The first and greatest problem, it seems to me, is that the scriptures come to the average layperson most frequently through their attendance at the liturgy and through their own devotional life. This is not a bad way to encounter the scriptures (indeed, the argument could be made that it is the best way), but the liturgical context of such scriptural encounters brings certain very real problems with it.

The first of these problems is that the language of scripture is heard as a familiar language in an all-too-familiar setting. In other words, it is from the vantage point of the pew that we expect to hear certain words at certain times and, if we are old enough, we have heard it all before—many times. The customary encounter with the scriptures in the ordinary times of worship breeds familiarity, and familiarity, while it sometimes breeds contempt, more often breeds boredom or a sense that we have heard it all before.

That boredom most commonly manifests itself in the sense that we know what the scriptures mean and what its vocabulary is trying to say. We know who the good Samaritan is, why the pharisees are not to be imitated, why we should avoid sin, and so forth. Those words and characters have echoed in our minds, reverberating off familiar walls in the air of familiar smells (of incense, beeswax, and Sunday clothes), filtered through the soft light of stained glass, and delivered in the same unction of the preacherly voice for years. We know the scriptures in the same way we know dental work: Both are done in contexts that are readily identifiable. Dental work conjures up Muzak, tattered magazines, and reassuring words of painlessness just as God and sin and grace trigger memories of the local parish. The words of revelation, to borrow an image from the novelist Walker Percy, seem like poker chips worn thin through constant use.

How, then, do we connect the comfortable words of grace with life apart from the experience of church? That the problem is a genuine one can be tested by the simple act of transposing the language of church (which is the language of the Bible) to a somewhat alien setting. Biblical words of pardon take on a new resonance and urgency when remembered in a prison, just as the language of forgiveness and "turning the other cheek" mock us when we are in the middle of a family feud (never mind loving your enemies, the Communists.

What about your odious, bad-mouthed cousin?). These are somewhat moralistic examples, but they do let us see to what degree our very churchgoing habits have domesticated the power of the scriptures. How, in effect, are we hearing these words or, more to the point, not hearing them?

We should be clear at this juncture of the various ways in which the Bible becomes the focus of interpretation. Very schematically (and relying somewhat on an old but useful work on this topic, Dom Charlier's *The Christian Approach to the Bible*) we can say that within the Christian community the Bible is approached in one of a number of different (but overlapping) ways:

> • *Theological exegesis*: the exhaustive study of the Bible both with scientific tools (philology, etc.) and as a subject for detailed theological reflection. This enterprise can either focus on the text itself and its meaning or, as a second step, how that text becomes formalized in the history of the tradition in various theological forms. Technical exegesis is an ongoing and absolutely crucial enterprise in the church because, as someone remarked, bad history almost always produces bad theology.
>
> • *Meditative reading*: making use of technical exegesis but focusing on the entire story of the Bible for either doctrinal or spiritual nourishment. This reading should culminate in what Charlier calls a *sapiential* reading in which the reader goes beyond understanding and faith to rest in love. It is at that point that the reader makes his or her reading into a prayer or into prayer itself.

This act of sapiential reading might be the effort of a single person as an act of devotion or it can be thought of as the collective exercise of the church as it listens, and responds to, the proclamation of the scriptures in its teaching and in its worship. While those acts are distinct they are not fully separable, much less antagonistic.

The average Catholic might feel that the task of reading the Bible in a sapiential manner is beyond the ken of those who do not have an enormous amount of background or a will to gain such background. That feeling of inadequacy should be disabused if for no other reason than the fact that God did not reveal himself in order to provide experts or specialists with material for graduate seminars. All are able to approach the Word of God and to approach it prayerfully. In fact, we should remind ourselves, as I have noted earlier in this chapter, that we do encounter the scriptures in the context of prayer since, most typically, we hear the scriptures in the liturgy—in worship.

At the risk of undue repetition let me emphasize once again that it is in the liturgy where we most appropriately meet the scriptures. In fact, as Luis Alonso-Schokel and others have indicated, what was read in the liturgy in the early church became a criterion for what was to be the canon of scripture. It is for this reason that in its deliberations on the liturgy the Second Vatican Council said, in its decree on the liturgy, that not only does God speak to us in the liturgy but also that "Christ is still proclaiming his gospel," which impels the faithful to respond in "hymn and prayer" (Constitution on the Sacred Liturgy, art. 33).

How can we recover the power of the scriptures to become prayer for us beyond the formal usages that we normally find in the scriptures? There is a hint in the church's tradition that may give us some help in this regard. I refer to the old monastic practice of lectio divina—the spiritual reading of the scriptures on a regular and prayerful basis.

It should be made clear that when I refer to lectio divina I am not talkiing about formal Bible study, nor even that sustained encounter with the scriptures which monks and nuns enjoy in the early morning intervals between the night office and the morning liturgy. My interest involves a consideration of the practice and goals of lectio divina conceived as broadly as is legitimate.

In his now classic study The Love of Learning and the Desire for God, Dom Jean Leclercq set out the authentic meaning of the monastic encounter with the scriptures. That encounter involved lectio-meditatio-oratio. The terms have a certain fluency but the dynamics go something like this: We need to hear and/or encounter the words of scripture (this is lectio broadly understood) and learn to savor and absorb them into our lives (*meditatio*) so that our lives, nourished on this continual encounter with the word of God, turn habitually to God (*oratio*). *Oratio* is understood in its deepest sense: as *contemplatio*. That turning to God, fueled by scriptural nourishment, compels us to turn once again to the scriptures (which are, after all, inexhaustible) for *lectio* and the cycle continues. The traditional monastic commentators assumed, as a matter of course, that this process was one that should engage the person throughout the course of a lifetime. The ultimate goal of such reading was to absorb the Word of God into our lives in such a way that this absorption should become the shaping instrument defining who we are and what we hope to be.

It is not difficult to see how this process of holy reading functioned in the monastic life. The constant nourishment of the liturgy provided the *lectio* even if one did very little independent reading. "Meditation" on those readings, when done as a part of the daily discipline of monastic living, should then "spill over" into affective prayer as a natural consequence. It is this system of nourishment that, ideally speaking, linked together the public worship of the monastery and the private contemplative growth of the monk or nun. Indeed, the traditional problem of the relationship of contemplation and liturgy can best be understood by a consideration of this interaction of *lectio* as linked with the liturgy and the natural overflow of that activity into constant prayer outside the formal prayer times.

But what has this to do with the average churchgoer?

One might first note that the principles that are assumed in the practice of *lectio divina*. According to a recent writer (Gerard MacGinty; cf. the reading list at the end of this chapter) the monastic theorists all agreed that the scriptures are addressed *to us, to me, here and now*; that the scriptures have a spiritual sense; that the true sense of scriptures come to us as a gift of the Holy Spirit; that one must cultivate an integral life if one is to find the fruits of scripture; and, finally, that the scriptures must be *savored* in a spirit of prayerful silence and recollection. Those presuppositions seem to me equally applicable to everyone and not simply for those virtuosi who embrace the contemplative life in a formal manner.

It would seem to me that one could adapt *lectio divina* to the circumstances of the ordinary Catholic (and it is the ordinary Catholic who concerns me) with great profit. I should like, first, to sketch out how this might be done and then, secondly, describe what appears to me to be some merits of this practice.

We shall allow *lectio* to stand for our customary encounter with the scriptures in the ordinary round of the liturgy: We go to church on Sunday and, more or less, hear the liturgy. We might even follow the scriptural pericopes by reading along in the missalette (a ghastly word!) provided for us. At this stage of encounter we are faced with a welter of words that are familiar (those words which remain the same week in and week out; e.g., the Lord's Prayer) and a bit strange (the cycle of readings from the lectionary) since they change each week. Now it is obvious that one cannot cope with all of these words with their diverse settings (prayers, exhortations, petitions, hymns, etc.) and their different sentiments. Nor is it always clear, unless one has a panoramic grasp of the scriptures, what the readings are about since they come to us in small doses and not always in context. As a beginning, then, we can say that the paramount encounter with the scriptures, however imperfectly grasped, comes in the community of worship.

It is possible, then, to isolate a single phrase from the entire liturgy that could become the focus of one's attention. One can begin the process of *lectio* by thinking small, not large. What I have in mind is something like this: from the entire liturgy a phrase be chosen that would become the subject of *meditatio*. Let us say, to use a random example, that we hear the Gospel account of the person who cries out to Jesus: "I believe, Lord. Help my unbelief." Would it not be possible to take that phrase and make it the subject of one's prayers for the week, i.e., until we return again on Sunday to worship? During that week the phrase would become part of one's prayers for morning and evening. It could become the short prayer we could turn to randomly throughout the week. It may well trigger in us a desire to expand that pithy sentiment so that we take to God our doubts and our weak faith; in such a case, *meditatio* turns, almost naturally, into *oratio*. It may be that such a phrase becomes such a powerful prayer for us that we will not abandon it but keep it as a prayer for life.

The ideal would be to keep those accumulated weekly prayers and add others from our encounter with the liturgy. It may well be that some people would even compose, either mentally or in a book, an anthology of such prayers from the scriptures or from the liturgy. Such phrases need not be technical, literal scriptural phrases. One could choose fragments from the eucharistic prayers of the liturgy that are redolent of scriptural sentiments. It is hard to think of any such line that does not have roots in the scriptures. For those who live in a family setting, it might even be useful to have one member of the family each week choose a phrase from the liturgy that could be the versicle for the prayer before meals each evening. The ways of multiplying these usages seem endless.

It would seem to me that the value of such a practice would be manifold. In the first place, it would link the public worship of the church with one's own personal spiritual life. It would overcome that dichotomy between liturgy and contemplation which so often worries both writers on spirituality and their readers. At this point it seems opportune to insert a favorite crochet of mine, which is that too much contemporary spirituality detaches itself from the ordinary public worship of the believing community.

My conviction is that not only does the practice I have outlined above allow for the most natural connection of scripture and prayer in a genuinely Catholic Christian manner but, properly developed, enhances both liturgy and private spiritual development. It is obviously not *the* way of Christian prayer, but it is *a* way in which a person can connect the Word of God with the passage of daily life. Furthermore, it provides a link between formal liturgy at the beginning of the week (Sunday is, after all the first day of the week) and the unfolding of the quotidian chores of Monday though Saturday.

Most importantly, however, it may aid in recovering the power of scriptural language to mold and shape us on life journeys. It does not seem wildly impossible that one might collect such prayer fragments into a personal anthology of prayer over the long haul. As one assimilates (through *meditatio*) the language of the scriptures in prayer (*oratio*), the language of the Bible, as it is encountered in the formal prayer of devotion of liturgy, may well take on a new urgency and thickness. It may even drive us to a more formal approach to the great story of the scriptures as the church unfolds it in the cycles of the liturgy. That would be a great gain, since it would not be an ideal to mine the scriptures for prayer in an atomistic manner to the detriment of an encounter with the great story of salvation that the scriptures manifest to us.

In *The Catholic Experience* I argued that the life of the Christian involves the telling of three stories: the story of salvation proclaimed in the person of Jesus Christ, proclaimed as a story in the unfolding life of the church juxtaposed to our story as lived in that tradition. The great challenge of the Christian life is to see those stories not as discrete and separate but as facets of one narrative that involves the presence of grace in the world of actuality past and present. At this level of things we are moving beyond the practice of using this or that verse of scripture as a springboard for prayer. We begin now to listen to the great story of salvation as it touches our own personal story.

In that sense, the prayer life of a Christian is not to be construed as a series of fits and starts in which one passes from the ordinary business of living into moments of prayer neatly demarcated from that living. The life of the Christian is a series of conversions in which the old person is renewed and transformed through an ongoing encounter with the Word of God as proclaimed and celebrated in the life of the church. That process is variously described in the New Testament as "Christ who lives in me" (Gal. 2:20) or the "surpassing worth of knowing Christ Jesus" (Phil. 3:7), or any of those other Pauline phrases in which the old person is transformed unto the likeness of Christ.

The fact that we most commonly encounter the scriptures in the formal setting of the liturgy does not mean that the scriptures cannot nourish us apart from that setting. My emphasis on the liturgical setting and the possible extensions of it derives from my impression that it is there in the liturgy that most Catholics will make their initial contact with the Word of God. On that impression I built my first suggestion(s) about connecting the proclamations of the liturgy with the ongoing life of prayer.

The conspicuous success of the base Christian communities of Latin America and elsewhere shows us that a Bible-centered paraliturgical setting can be designed which is nonelitist, spiritually nourishing, and potentially powerful in its capacity to transform the lives of people. Base Christian communities seem inextricably entwined with liberation theology (or better, liberation theologies, since there are many of them), and the merits or shortcomings of that particular theology are not something that I wish to discuss here. It is clear, however, that a good deal of the nourishment of those theologies derive from the lived experience of large numbers of people who gather in small, manageable communities to read the scriptures in a prayerful setting with the express purpose of listening to the scriptures and then, as a necessary second step, to inquire how those things meditated on and learned can be applied to the business of ordinary life.

Now, it seems to me, that a good deal of what one learns from the prayerful study of the scriptures in a communal setting is going to depend on who is in the community, from what strata of the populace the community is drawn up, and how people in that community understand themselves and the situation(s) in which they find themselves. Thus, to cite an obvious example, if one reads that Jesus says that it is far easier for a camel to pass through the eye of a needle than for a rich person to enter the Kingdom of heaven, one is going to see that story somewhat differently if one lives on the upper East Side of New York or if one lives, unemployed, in an urban slum in Central America. Both, if one allows for a basic sense of fairness, might conclude that a man can be just and rich but each group might radically differ as to how the rich person can or should handle his riches vis-à-vis the vast sea of the poor. Similarly, a person who is relatively well to do might pray for "peace of mind," while one who is in grinding poverty might pray, simply, for food to succor one's children. Nobody, in short, can read the scriptures independently of the culture in which he or she lives. While it might be argued that a particular text has a fundamental "meaning," it is equally clear that it has many meanings when it is read in an existential context. That is true because, as contemporary critics never tire of saying, we read the text but the text also reads us.

This difference in social setting is noted not to insist that the fruits of prayerful reading of the scriptures are hopelessly relativized, but to be clear that reading and prayer are not done in a timeless vacuum of abstraction. It is also to note that the constraints on social or class interpretations of the Bible are to be found in the general witness of the Christian tradition in time and space. That is not to say that new insights cannot be found in the reading of the scriptures. It is very much to say that no new insight can be put forward that clearly is dissonant with what the community has always held. The Catholic reading of the Bible cannot accept the notion of a radically individualistic approach to the Bible, whether done by an individual per se or by a sectarian community cut off from the great church in time and space. The communal reading of the scriptures in a sapiential fashion must also be a Catholic reading of the scriptures. It is well to remember that every Sunday Christians of very different cultures and conditions listen to the same readings and attempt to wrestle meanings from them.

To insist on a Catholic reading of the scripture is a healthy corrective to what may be called the "fundamentalist temptation." The fundamentalist temptation, presented to us either by an aggressive missionary effort or as a natural desire for absolute certitude, has this common feature: the desire to see the Bible as a supernatural *book* that, like the ancient oracles of the Greeks and Romans, holds secrets, promises, hints, and solutions to whatever issue may be at hand. Most of all, the fundamentalist sees the Bible as a *book*—something that stands as an objective, tactile thing which holds within its concrete reality Truth. Finally, it is to see that book in a rarefied relationship in which there is only me and that *book* free from any sense of the communal sharing of that book or the constraints of the tradition which nourishes it and protects it. The fundamentalist goes to the Bible as if it were a medicine chest: full of disparate remedies but each useful for a specific malady.

The ultimate logic of the fundamentalist temptation is to isolate the book as a norm to which the believing person must approach as an outsider who seeks its truth. I say "ultimate logic," but it is a logic that does appear. A Catholic reading of the Bible insists, on the contrary, that scripture is the church's book both in the sense that the scriptures are born in the church and the church, in turn, protects, seeks to understand, reaches up, and constantly meditates on its truth. We may—indeed, should—read the scriptures as individuals but never in a way that blocks out or erases the common memory of those who, as a community, have listened and responded to that reading as a worshiping body of witnesses in time and space.

A Catholic prays in the words of scripture, in the spirit of what the scriptures teach but, ultimately, not with the scriptures as a model. The model is Jesus the Christ whom the scriptures proclaim. A sapiential reading of the scriptures sees them as leading to Christ, proclaiming him in his salvific mission, and promising us the reality of his presence until, as Saint Paul says, he comes again. We read the Hebrew scriptures because Jesus read and listened to them and bears witness to their truth; we read the Christian scriptures because they tell us who Jesus was and what the community of first memories believed about him and what Jesus believed about his own past.

A prayerfully Catholic reading of the scriptures is, at base, a christological reading of the scriptures—a reading not designed for information, moral uplift, or history (although, obviously, it may provide all of those things) but a reading designed that we might believe that "Jesus is the Christ, the Son of God, and that believing you might have life in his name" (John 20:31). It is for that reason I think the recent emergence of what is called "canonical criticism" is to be applauded. Canonical criticism insists that scripture must be read and interpreted as a scripture of the church. Canonical criticism does not neglect the technical work of exegesis; indeed, it insists on it as a first step in giving an account of the scriptures as they have been understood in the ongoing life of the church. Canonical critics are most interested in the scriptures as a finished product. Exegesis, for such critics, arises, in the words of Brevard Childs—one of its most distinguished practitioners—as a "theological discipline within the context of the canon and is directed towards the community of faith which lives by its confession of Jesus Christ."

To the extent that canonical criticism becomes a trend in the Catholic community, we will see the reemergence of a spiritual reading of the scriptures which will combine a rigorous reading of the text with a profound sense of how that text lives in the community of belief. It will be a tradition that draws on the work of contemporary scholars as well as the inherited commentary tradition of the past. That kind of reading of the scriptures will make explicit what is tacit but constant in the liturgy, which is to say, the prayer life of the church: scripture as received by the church is a seamless web that looks back on itself and out to those who participate in its life.

There are emergent indications that the benign tyranny of the professional exegete who opts solely for a scientifically controlled interpretation of the text is coming to an end. However much we owe such exegesis (and it is a very great deal), there is a need to get back to that deeper sense of the text as a vehicle for the enrichment of the believing community. With an increased interest in the theological power of symbol, metaphor, narrative, etc., there is every hope that the older tradition of reading the scriptures will come, once again, to the fore, but this time nourished by the enormous advance made by historical-critical methods.

It is precisely the densely metaphoric sense of the Bible (its *polysemous*, or many-signifying, character, to borrow a term from Dante) that makes it inexhaustible for the praying Christian. It is possible to pray the Psalms in the spirit of the ancient Hebrews precisely because the Psalms reflect the God Jesus believed in. It is possible to meditate on the pericopes that deal with this or that incident in the life of Jesus precisely because the early community treasured those incidents and, for added measure, retold them in terms of their own faith and experience as believers in Jesus. The fundamentalist mind might insist that those incidents are history, but as Northrup Frye has recently written, it is their historicity that is most irrelevant to their meaning. When one tries to reach back to pure history, one finds more often than not echos and allusions to the earlier tradition of the Bible or the faith practices of the community that created and preserved the stories themselves. Frye, as a literary critic, argues what the church has always instinctively taught: the Bible is endlessly self-referential.

The multilayered character of the Bible must also be contrasted with its silences. One of the exercises that I have given my students is to ask them to read one of the Gospels (e.g., Mark) and then write an essay on what that Gospel does *not* tell us about Jesus that would be interesting to know. The suggestions that come back are as varied and as different as one can imagine. The point is (and it was made compellingly years ago in a famous essay by Eric Auerbach) that the Bible gives us very little "background" with which to operate. It is the reader who must fill in the specific horrors of the passion narratives or the appearance of the risen Christ. Most of us, one suspects, fill in a good deal of that background through the agency of remembered artistic representations.

Just as we can pray in the words of scripture so we can also pray in the silences of scriptures. To put it another way, we can enter into the witness of the Bible as participants, filling up those gaps that are left to us. This is an ancient and hallowed practice in the Christian tradition. Its most common form is through the use of ritual. The passion narratives are a case in point. Everything from the stations of the cross to the Holy Week processions of Hispanic countries (to the more demanding rituals of the *penitentes* of Mexico) are an attempt to flesh out and identify with the story that the New Testament provides for us. Yet, such rituals are not a mere pantomime of action; they are also an acting out of certain Pauline formulations that encourage one to be crucified with Christ or otherwise participate in his redemptive death. Nor, just to make an obvious point, are such practices all that distant phenomenologically from the eucharistic liturgy itself, which has often been described as the sacred "drama of the Mass."

The ritualizing of parts of scriptures are attempts to flesh out the narrative line to make the "story" more real, more applicable, and more existential. In that sense, the entire sacramental life of the church can be seen as a kind of dramatic prayer with the central script being provided by the scriptures themselves. Sacramental gestures, which are interpreted in the light of the scriptural tradition, as the ritual books make clear, are not only channels of grace and signs of God's presence. They are, preeminently, acts of worship. They are also, simultaneously, a commentary on scripture and a meditation on its spiritual meaning.

Another way in which the scriptures are extended into forms of prayer is through the use of scripture (selectively interpreted) as a model for an entire way of life. The entire history of monasticism and ascetic living is patterned on a response to a certain emphasis in the New Testament whose great themes are solitary prayer, self-bnegation, freely embraced poverty, and the desert experience of wrestling with the demonic and the naked encounter with God. The monastic desire for transformation is, after all, simply a desire to put into living reality the dictum of Paul that "I live, now not I; but Christ lives in me."

I use the example of monasticism, but is not that form of paradigmatic living simply the often-cited need to live after the example of Christ writ large or writ more dramatically? After all, it is said that the goal of the entire Christian life is to live after the manner of Christ. That translates into a demand that somehow our lives conform, however imperfectly, to the life of Christ who is preached to us from the New Testament in the churches.

We should be aware of how rich the Catholic tradition is in giving us models for this *imitatio Christi*. Indeed, when one looks at this tradition (as Jaroslav Pelikan has recently done in *Jesus Through the Centuries*) it is evident that there is no single biblical manner that is imitable. What one possesses are many strains in the scriptures that allow us to construct a manner of imitation. Thus, to generalize, the imitation of

Christ meant one thing in late medieval Europe and quite another thing in nineteenth-century America.

This desire to incarnate the scriptures takes many forms. In
the life of Saint Francis of Assisi, we see Francis as attempting to flesh out Christ's counsels of poverty in an absolutely
literal manner (if there ever was a fundamentalist it was Saint
Francis; his fundamentalism, like all fundamentalisms, was,
however, selective) or, in the famous incident of the stigmata
on Mt. LaVerna, actually becoming what the Gospels tell us
of Jesus in his passion. The imitation of Christ in the life of
Francis was, to borrow Ewert Cousins's useful formulation,
the mysticism of a historical event. In a certain and precise
sense we can say that what Francis achieved in his life was a
fusion of word and gesture so that he became a living exemplar of the crucified Christ.

Francis is one of those classics of the tradition (to borrow
David Tracy's characterization) to whom we intuitively turn,
but the larger truth is that the entire tradition of the spiritual
masters and mistresses of our heritage can be viewed as an
attempt to live out the life of Christ in some palpably real
and compelling manner. In that attempt, we conclude, life becomes prayer itself.

How does that enfleshment of the Christ of the scriptures
take concrete form in our own day and time? There is no obvious single answer to that question, but certain generalities
are not out of order. First, there is no absolute dichotomy
with the past. It is a conceit of every age that its uniqueness
demands no reverence toward the past. That was not, and is
not now, true. In fact, when we look at the great spiritual figures of our own day we see both continuity with the past and
adjustments demanded by the pressures peculiar to our own
age. Thus, a Teilhard de Chardin reflects a desire to grapple
with the challenges of the scientific and post-scientific
age, but his spirituality is unthinkable without reference to
the sapiential tradition of Christology with its echos of the
Greek patristic tradition and its penetrating reflections on
the cosmic Christ of Pauline theology. A similar case could
be made for any other notable spiritual figure that one cares
to name.

The dialectic of past/present that one finds in the spiritual masters and mistresses is a reflection of the same dialectic which is at work in the church's meditations on the scriptures. It is impossible, even if one attempts to bracket consciously the weight of the past, to read the scriptures without the background of two millennia of commentary, formulation, and explication. We have absorbed that background so completely that we are often not aware of it. When we hear the words of scripture, we hear words not in an abstract fashion but words that have been proclaimed and uttered by generations of the believing community. When we seek to understand, we seek, however implicitly, to understand not simply the text but the significances added to those words over the centuries.

The lessons for prayer to be gleaned from the density of biblical language are profound. One thing that is obvious is that the words of prayer which we use so handily and so familiarly are worthy of reflection because they carry with them immense meaning and great weight. Secondly, if we can grasp that depth in the words, we slowly learn to pray not only as individuals or members of a community in the here and now but also in communion with those who have uttered those same words and sentiments in our common past. Finally, those words are revelatory, which is to say that they pull back the veils and give us some glimpse into the mystery which is God. To pray in the words of Christ, to be specific, is to link ourselves with the One who knows God in a unique and unmatchable manner. To use those words gives us at least a partial entry into that unique relationship with God and, since we must always think of this as Catholic prayer, with those others who pray in the same words and the same Spirit.

A Prayer

Let us keep the scriptures ever in mind and meditate upon them day and night, persevering in prayer, always on the watch.

Let us beg the Lord to give us real knowledge of what we read and to show us not only how to understand it but how to put it into practice, so that we might obtain spiritual grace,

enlightenment by the law of the Holy Spirit, through Jesus
Christ our Lord, whose power and glory will endure through-
out the ages.
Amen.

This prayer is attributed to the greatest of the Greek Fathers, Origen (184?–254?). Much of what would become commonplaces in ascetical and mystical theology has its roots in
his powerful commentaries on the sacred scriptures to which
he devoted his indefatigable energies. As many commentators
have noted, Origen never saw the reading of the Bible as an
academic exercise. It was a religious exercise in which the
deepest meaning of the scriptures demands a mystical language to express its thoughts. As Andrew Louth noted in a
recent book, Origen enters more deeply into communion
with God as a result of his engagement with scriptures.

The short prayer we cite above makes a number of points
that are central to the concerns of this chapter. Origen links
the encounter of scriptures with the life of prayer and the discipline of the spiritual life. Furthermore, he begs God to give
him *understanding* which, for Origen, means that sense of
the Bible which stands behind the obvious (or not so obvious!) literal meaning of the text. Finally, that prayerful discovery of the truth of the scriptures should lead us not only to a
closer relationship with God but also refine and reshape our
lives. That new relationship with God and the world comes
from the impetus of the Holy Spirit as we pray in solidarity
with Jesus Christ.

This prayer comes from a selection of prayers to be read be-
fore studying the Bible found in *The New Book of Christian
Prayers*, edited by Tony Castle (New York: Crossroad, 1986).
For a summary of recent writings on this seminal figure, see
Henri Crouzel, "The Literature on Origen: 1970–1988," *Theo-
logical Studies* 49 (1988), pp. 499–516.

A Note on Readings

The classic work on *lectio divina* is Jean LeClercq's *The
Love of Learning and the Desire for God* (New York: Fordham

University Press, 1961). To that I would add Gerard MacGinty's "Lectio Divina: Fount and Guide of the Spiritual Life," *Cistercian Studies* 21 (1986), pp. 64–71. Some of the ideas in this section have been treated in another context in my *The Catholic Experience* (New York: Crossroad, 1985).

Two older books on the Bible that have been useful to me are Dom Celestin Charlier's *The Christian Approach to the Bible* (London: Sands, 1958) and Luis Alonso-Schokel's *The Inspired Word: Scripture in the Light of Language and Literature* (New York: Herder and Herder, 1965). The dated nature of their discussions makes it clear how badly we need a full study of the scriptures as a book of the church, especially in its life of worship. Jean Daniélou's *The Bible and the Liturgy* (Notre Dame, IN: Notre Dame University Press, 1956) is still valuable for its understanding of typology but does not take into account the reforms of Vatican II.

Northrop Frye's *The Great Code: The Bible and Literature* (New York: Harcourt, Brace and Jovanovich, 1982) has splendid pages on both the denseness of biblical language and the unity of that language. I have been impressed by the enterprise of Brevard Childs in such books as *The Book of Exodus: A Critical Theological Commentary* (Philadelphia: Westminster, 1974) and *Introduction to the Old Testament as Scriptures* (Philadelphia: Fortress, 1979), which both make a case for canonical criticism.

The literature on Christian base communities, as is clear from a perusal of Maryknoll's Orbis publications, is enormous. One detailed study of such communities in Brazil is very thorough and helpful: Marcello de C. Azevedo's *Basic Ecclesial Communities in Brazil: The Challenge of a New Way of Being Church* (Washington, DC: Georgetown University Press, 1987).

Jaroslav Pelikan's *Jesus Through the Centuries* (New Haven, CN: Yale University Press, 1985) has an interesting chapter on Franciscan *imitatio Christi*; the classic study is Ewert Cousins, "Francis of Assisi: Christian Mysticism at the Crossroads," in *Mysticism and Religious Traditions*, edited by Steven T. Katz (New York: Oxford University Press, 1983), pp. 163–90.

The profound relationship between Bible and spirituality in the early period of the church is traced out in some detail in Andrew Louth's *The Origins of the Christian Mystical Tradition* (Oxford: Clarendon Press, 1981); cf. also Sandra Schneiders, "Scripture and Spirituality," in *Christian Spirituality: Origins to the Twelfth Century*, edited by Bernard McGinn, et al. (New York: Crossroad, 1985). Louis Bouyer's *A History of Christian Spirituality*, 3 vols. (New York: Seabury, 1982), keeps a steady eye on the biblical roots of the tradition of spirituality.

5

JESUS

Behold, the Lord is our mirror.
Open your eyes and see them in him.

The Odes of Solomon

Ideally, this book should begin (and, for that matter, end) with the subject of Jesus who is called the Christ. It is Jesus, after all, who not only stands at the center of the entire Christian enterprise but stands in such a way that without him Christianity not only has no name but no meaning. Remove Jesus from direct and central consideration and any book that pretends to deal with Catholic prayer implodes in on the nothingness of its own hollow center. Christian prayer, like Christianity itself, must constantly return to the figure of Jesus. Not to do so is to invite idolatry and ideology, as Dostoevsky warned us in the legend of the Grand Inquisitor. We take our stand with some compelling words of Karl Rahner:

> Jesus becomes, in this love of ours for him, the concrete Absolute, in whom the abstractness of norms, and the insignificance of the purely contingent individual, are transcended and overcome.

It is on that concrete Absolute that we focus in this chapter. This chapter finds itself near the center of the present work because all we have said hitherto presupposes Jesus while everything said subsequently derives from what is made explicit

90

here. Still, it is obvious, once that centrality has been as-
serted, that we can do more than skim lightly over the surface
of a vast and complex topic. Such superficiality is inevitable
both because Jesus is inexhaustible mystery (a theological
reason) and because the whole history of Catholic prayer finds
its source in the paradigmatic actions of Jesus (a practical reason). Nonetheless, from the tangled skein of our chapter subject, we hope to draw out a few threads to highlight some of
the basic theses of this entire work.

As an introduction to this chapter we can recall the opening assertions of this book and reiterate that Jesus is, *par excellence*, a pray-er. This is true at the most rudimentary level,
because the Catholic tradition has, in the most variegated
forms, attempted to give concrete expression to the prayer life
of Jesus as it appears to us in the Gospels. Where would the
organized prayer life of the church and the contemplative
strains in Catholicism be if we did not have the evangelical
witness which tell us that Jesus went out to lonely places to
pray (Mark 1:35) or retired to that *axis mundi*, the mountaintop (Mark 14:23) or the desert (Luke 5:16) to commune with
the Father? The hermitages, deserts, monasteries, and retreats
of historic Catholicism are all enfleshments of those brief
lines from the Gospels. It would be a wonderful, if daunting,
enterprise simply to isolate little phrases from the Gospels
(e.g., the injunction to "pray always") and trace the entire tra-
dition(s) of spirituality that emanate from them. It might be
worth noting, just to cite one example from many, that the
Flemish mystic, John Ruusbroec (1293–1381), composed his
entire mystical treatise *The Spiritual Espousals* by an extended meditation on a single verse from the Gospel of Matthew: "See, the bridegroom is coming. Go out to meet him"
(25:6). This is something we will insist on, to the point of
repetition, because it drives home the important truth that
much derives from single instances in the scripture that take
on full significance not as simply read but as acted out and
enfleshed in the circumstances of spiritual living.

Similarly, the theological treatises on prayer and the contemplative literature has been built out of equally terse verses
of the Gospels. How much has the quality and character of

prayer been influenced by the warnings of Jesus against mere formality in prayer? (See Matt. 6:5–8, 15:8–9.) How many insights into perseverance in prayer and the efficacy of such perseverance been gained by the simple and direct faith of Jesus in his naked insistence that "whatever you ask in prayer, you will receive it, if you have faith" (Matt. 21:22)? Is it not likewise true that the sacramental gestures (understood in the widest possible sense of the term) have been enhanced by the long meditation of the church on the Jesus who lays his hands on children and prays (Matt. 19:13)? Is not the mystical literature of the church constantly enriched by the great theophanies like that of the Transfiguration when Jesus and the disciples go to the mountain to pray (Luke 9:28)? How much has the ascetic life been influenced by the passion narratives and the theology of the cross found in the writings of Paul?

These vignettes (and many more like them) from the synoptics, at times recorded as almost *obiter dicta*, have given rise to a whole literature and various styles of prayer in the church. One of the extraordinary things about the history of Christian spirituality is that it is possible to isolate a single verse or incident from the scriptures and trace, from that verse, an entire tradition of prayer in the church. What has saved the church from a mindless fundamentalism in this enterprise is the traditional awareness that such avenues of prayer always need testing against other Gospel values. The entire tension between contemplation and action can be seen as a discussion which derives from the image of Jesus in solitary prayer in the desert set against the same Jesus who speaks and heals amid the swirl and clangor of village life. The hermeneutics of spiritual development is a persistent appropriation of the smaller that is tested against the larger.

It should also be said, though the point needs no special emphasis, that this process by which a Gospel vignette becomes the source for a spiritual tradition is not simpleminded fundamentalism, even though such texts may be fundamental for this or that spiritual tradition. While we respond to the Word of God as a simple Word, that Word is also heard through the discrete words of sacred scripture as they are proclaimed in the church. The part can stand for the whole or at least as an entry to the whole. We never fully encompass all the words of the Gospel, but those words can be the trigger for the embracing of the Word. The spiritual tradition provides ample proof of that. There is a line that runs from Anthony of the Desert through Augustine to Francis of Assisi down to Francis Xavier where a radical and specific form of life emerges as a result of simply hearing a passage of the Gospel proclaimed. In all of those instances— and many like them—the change is, in the first instance, a change to a life of deep prayer and a life of action however differently acted out.

Jesus, then, and the things said about Jesus, make him a paradigm, *the* paradigm of the pray-er. Yet, there is a deeper sense in which we can approach Jesus as pray-er, and that sense brings us to the Trinitarian dynamic of our faith in general and our life of prayer in particular. Put succinctly, the prayer of Jesus derives its unique and compelling character from his profound sense in the Spirit that he addresses *Abba*. Contemporary theologians have isolated that relationship— the *Abba* experience—as the crucial datum for an understanding of Jesus and, by extension, our understanding of being in Jesus: Jesus prays to *Abba* in the Spirit.

It has been often noted that *Abba* (the word is Aramaic) denotes a peculiarly intimate form of address to a beloved parent. I have resisted the suggestion that the term should be translated as "Daddy" as being too jarringly vulgar. Nor does the phrase "dear father" (suggested by Joachim Jeremias) escape the echo of middle-class respectability. *Abba* does not translate easily into acceptable English and should be allowed to stand in the original to give us some sense of the language of Jesus himself. We need to understand it as a term of endearment which comprehends that intimate bond existing between parent and child in the most loving of family arrangements. *Abba* itself remained in the early Christian community as a talismanic word (see Rom. 8:15 and Gal. 4:6) for God and, following that example, it should stand in its original form for us. The very fact that the Aramaic word *"Abba"* lingers in the New Testament literature is indication that it holds, in its four letters, an echo of the voice of Jesus himself.

The basic lesson of the *Abba* experience, found both in the prayer and in the life of Jesus, is that our relationship to that which is ultimate is a bond which is personal, intimate, and loving. At this level, then, we can say that our prayer, considered either formally as discourse with God explicitly or informally as the life of faith, roots itself in the deep conviction that we are loved, nourished, and fulfilled in this world. That sense of intimate bonding is at the core of the experience of Jesus. It constitutes the foundation for our conviction that Jesus is the preeminent pray-er.

We say that this experience is Trinitarian because the New Testament links in an indissoluble whole the single image of Jesus (and, by extension, us) as uttering *Abba* in the Spirit. We might recall Paul's assertion that "God has sent the Spirit of his Son into our hearts crying '*Abba*! Father!' " (Gal. 4:6). There the Trinitarian circle is complete in the actual economy of life: God sends the resurrected Christ into us by the Spirit so that we can call God, not God, but *Abba*. If our contention is correct, this is not only an affirmation of faith ("God is *Abba*") but an utterance of prayer in faith.

There is yet another point. Although it is true, as James Mackey and others have noted, that it is Luke alone who singles out Jesus as a model of prayer, it is likewise true that the prayer experience of Jesus figures in all the Gospel accounts and preeminently so in John. A close examination of the prayer of Jesus as it reveals itself in the Gospels shows an intimate connection between the "character" of Jesus and his mission. That point has been made so compellingly by Walter Kasper that he deserves to be quoted in full:

> Because Jesus' faith and love are embodied in his prayer, that prayer is our clearest sight of the unity of Jesus' nature and mission. A request is an admission of poverty. Someone who makes a request places himself in the power of another person. In his obedience, Jesus is an empty mold for God; in his faith he is a mode of existence of the love of God. Because he is the one who believes totally, he is the person who is totally filled with God's power, he shares in God's almighty power, which consists of love. But by being totally open to God, he is totally open to us. Being petitioner makes him at the same time Lord. If making a request is the mark of poverty and powerlessness,

being able to make a request is proof of a power and potential which must be given by another. Poverty and wealth, power and helplessness, fulness and emptiness, receptivity and completion are embodied in Jesus. His nature as the son is inseparable from his mission and destiny. His is God's existence for others.

The characterization of Jesus given above is not filled, as it might appear at first reading, with paradox. The polarities that Kasper suggests (poverty/wealth, fulness/emptiness, etc.) constitute a *coincidentia oppositorum* that resolves itself in the deeper union of what subsequent theology would call the hypostatic union. Another way of expressing this somewhat daring truth is that it is exactly in his role of petitioner that Jesus has the power to grant and in his emptying (his *kenosis*, in the language of theology) that he is filled. This, as I say, is not merely the paradox of the mystic but the only way in which Jesus can be described in a dynamic fashion. To hold on to the power of that dynamic is to steer away from the temptation to divinize Jesus at the expense of his radical earthiness, just as it is a safeguard against trivializing the transcendent claims that the church has always made about Jesus.

To hold in equilibrium these polarities is not always easy. We are all the heirs of the christological formulations that have come down to us from the Council of Chalcedon in the fifth century. The emphasis on the divinity of Jesus as a sign of orthodox belief has not always been matched by a concomitant emphasis on his humanity. A good deal of the reflexive fear of modern scriptural studies can be traced to a deep aversion to "tinkering" with the safe image of Jesus the Christ as it is formulated in the creeds. At the back of many minds is the fear (not always irrational) that the desire to "demystify" the Gospels is, in effect, a program that reduces Jesus to a shadowy figure of late antique Judaism sanitized from any right to transcendent claims.

We can see the dimensions of this problem by posing this simple question: do we pray *to* Jesus or *with* him?

It is obvious that to ask that question is to ask the question about Jesus as the Son of God with all of the theological implications implicit in our faith formulations of him as true man and true God. The short answer to the question as we have posed it is answered, of course, in the prayer practice of the church. We need go no further than the eucharistic liturgy for our answer. Each of the prefatory remarks of the four eucharistic prayers of the Roman liturgy address God directly but *through* the person of Jesus Christ. The beginning of Eucharistic Prayer I is typical:

> We come to you, Father
> with praise and thanksgiving
> through Jesus Christ your Son
> Through him we ask you to accept
> and bless
> these gifts we offer to you in sacrifice.

To paraphrase that canonical prayer is to say this: We adore God alone who is, as we know in grace and faith, triune but we offer that adoration through the agency of Jesus Christ who is God incarnate. And we do that in and through the power of the Spirit of God.

Can we specify more fully what we mean to say by the term *through*? Obviously, it carries a special meaning beyond mere agency. It is a hallowed part of the Catholic tradition to pray "through" the intercession of the Blessed Virgin and the saints. Our prayer language is filled with such sentiments (e.g., "All for Jesus through Mary"); so the role of Jesus in prayer cannot be reduced to the intercessory power of Jesus as a first among even unequals. The *through* of the liturgy means something quite different.

My suggestion would be that we understand that *through* in the light of Johannine faith where Jesus sets out the relationship of the Son to the Godhead: "Do you not believe that I am in the Father and the Father in me?" (John 14:10). "If a man loves me, he will keep my word, and my father will love him, and we will come to him, and make our home with him" (John 14:23). "For the Father has loved you because you loved me and have believed that I have come from the Father" (John 16:27). The simplest way to consider that relationship is to think of Jesus as the visible sign—the sacrament—of God's presence in the world of time and history. That is why Rahner's phrase of *concrete Absolute* is so telling: It locates Jesus in the world of history and contingency as an irreducible reality who "explains" not only history and the world but what transcends it.

We then look to Jesus as the one who most perfectly and most definitively shows us the way to adhere to God both in faith and in prayer. Jesus is not simply the model for that prayer but the one with whom we stand in our prayer to God. We can never pray with the sentiments of Jesus fully nor can we cultivate the bonds that he had to the Father. We can only approximate those sentiments and approach those bonds. It is precisely in that gap between the perfection of Jesus as pray-er and our own status that the natural urge to praise and emulate arises. To stand in companionship with Jesus before the Father is, simultaneously, to praise by acknowledgment and to join with him in adoration before God. In other words, no matter how haltingly, we stand with Jesus as our standard of prayer and join our prayer to his.

On this subject, as in so many others, Thomas Merton has some instructive things to say. In a little-noticed essay entitled "The Humanity of Christ in Monastic Prayer" (see the bibliography at the end of this chapter) Merton asks whether, at some stage in contemplative prayer, the meditated image of the humanity of Christ should be "let go" in order to experience the imageless reality of God. Merton is quick to point out the condemnations of Molinos and the other Quietists of the seventeenth century who thought that contemplation should be pure without the presence of person or attributes of God, or that acts of love toward the humanity of Christ (or the saints or Mary) were bad because they were sensible sentiments toward sensible images in the mind. Obviously, Merton does not wish to fall into the trap of Quietism.

What Merton demonstrates, by reference to both patristic and medieval theologians, is that orthodox monastic theologians always taught that even in the most apophatic forms of prayer it was always something being done in the company of, through the example of, or in communion with the whole

Christ. The events in the human life of Jesus are worthy objects of love and admiration as well as incitements to prayers. Contemplation, however, does not stop there. Jesus dwells within us through grace and in his presence through faith. Thus, Merton concludes, the ultimate resting place of true prayer is the "light received in the inner depths of our being from the risen saviour, God and man, reigning in the glory of the Father."

What one finds in the Christian mystical tradition are two approaches (viae) to God. One, the apophatic tradition that runs from the Pseudo-Dionysius through *The Cloud of Unknowing*, constitutes itself by the ascent (strongly influenced by the Neoplatonic roots of its theory) which abolishes and/or negates all images. The other, a kataphatic tradition best exemplified in the Franciscan tradition, dwells on the image of Christ. As Ewert Cousins has argued in his many studies, this Franciscan ascent turns (as did Dante in the final vision of the *Paradiso*) to the incarnate Christ even as the mystic contemplates the unity and trinity of God.

The problem, then, is one of the imagination. Our prayer does not direct itself ultimately to an image of Christ imagined from the Gospel but through Christ to the ultimate ground of his being which is in the mystery of Godhead. One of the most penetrating approaches to that mystery is to be found in the theology of the icon as it has been formulated over the centuries in Eastern theology. Saint John Damascene and others articulated what would become a pillar of Orthodox faith: That because of the Incarnation it is proper to approach God as "depictable" because the Creator of the world took on flesh. Still, as the very style of icons suggest, the icon is a window into the ultimate mysteries of our salvation. One does not worship the image of Christ on the icon tablet; one "sees" *through* the icon to come face to face with the real mysteries of salvation. It has been wisely said by Orthodox theologians like Timothy Ware that the basic characteristic of Eastern Christian prayer can be summarized by the term "gazing." One need only think of that word in tandem with the function of icons to see the apt character of the observation. We see through the icon the depicted mysteries of faith.

Those depictions are, typically, anchored in the gold background of the icon itself. The gold background both hints at eternity and serves as a metaphoric sign of God (who "is light"). Through the icon, in short, we penetrate, however haltingly, to God.

We pray, then, *through* Christ, but also we pray *with* Christ. Again, we can reflect a bit on the simple preposition *with*. That reflection can be set out in the form of a question: "How do we pray *with* Christ?

At the most rudimentary level, we have already answered that question. We pray with Christ when we make his sentiments of prayer our own. In that sense, we try to reach up to the figure of Jesus in the New Testament and pray as he prayed both in terms of his suggested form of prayer (i.e., the Our Father) and after his fashion of praying: in community with others and as a solitary affirmation of relationship with *Abba*. That much is clear and has already been discussed.

We can further specify this prayer *with* Jesus by recalling an important observation of Maurice Nedoncelle in his still useful book, *God's Encounter with Man: A Contemporary Approach to Prayer*: "Prayer *in nomine Jesu* really gains its complete meaning only though belief in the presence of Jesus in the church. . . . Thus Christian prayer also has a relationship to the church and the sacraments as a distinctive characteristic." Prayer *with* Jesus, in short, has a profoundly ecclesiological dimension to it.

Church is never more church than in the moments when the believing community gathers to celebrate the liturgy. That ingathering of the community is done after the command of Christ, in his presence and in his name, and through that name and presence, Jesus is recalled, represented, recreated, and reenacted in time and space. Christ, in that sense, is the alpha and omega of all liturgical celebration. It is then that through word and sacrament the presence of Christ is made palpable. Without the presence of Jesus there is, quite simply, no liturgy. With Jesus, however, the liturgy becomes valid, witnessed, and efficacious.

The liturgy, like every act of common worship, has both a vertical and a horizontal dimension to it. Vertically, the community rises above itself to honor God *through* Christ; horizontally, the community bonds itself together in a corporate affirmation of Jesus as Christ to affirm that it is a *Christian* community. In both of those dimensions we are with Christ: as a part of the bond that he establishes as a community and acknowledging him as the mediatorial presence to the Father.

Wayne Meeks, in his influential work *The First Urban Christians: The Social World of the Apostle Paul*, has argued that the celebration of the Lord's Supper (as described in 1 Cor. 12) not only symbolized the unity of the early Christian boundary; it was also the eminent sign of the boundary between the believing community and its nonbelieving culture. For Meeks, the liturgy of the Pauline community sums up the unity of the Body of Christ as opposed to the chaos of the nonbelieving world with its "idol offerings." The believing community, in short, is *holy* in the sense that it is set apart by the precise mechanism of affirming Jesus the Christ as its center and *telos*. That "setting apart" does not imply, necessarily, sectarian resistance but rather the notion of what distinguished one social reality from another one.

One corollary that derives from the intense social bond established by the liturgy and the power of the liturgy to express that bond is this: No person who is in that community prays apart from Christ. On the negative side this means that whatever the subject of the prayer, how it is expressed, and to whom it is addressed, it is always in Christ because it is Christ who establishes the community which, after all, is called the Body of Christ. Positively, it means that consciously we pray in Christ, through him, and with him both in the formal utterances of the liturgy and as a kind of "spillover" from the liturgy.

Once we have fully grasped what it means to be a member of Christ's Body, which is the gathering community of believers, a number of "difficulties" with respect to prayer and Christ begin, if not to disappear, then surely to fit into this broader context. Thus, to cite an intense example, if someone prays at the level of the simple prayer of pure presence there is no indication that Christ has been "forgotten" or "eliminated" or "left behind." Nor do we need retreat into theological metaphysics to explain this prayer and its relationship to Christ. All we need do is remember that a believer, who prays in the quiet of simple prayer, by the very definition of being a believer, is praying with Christ and in him.

A specific example or two might make this point. In 1968 when Thomas Merton was on his Asian journey he spoke at a spiritual conference in Calcutta. At the end of his talk Merton led in a prayer that has been preserved in Appendix 5 of *The Asian Journal*. Here, in a somewhat abbreviated form, is that prayer:

> Oh God, we are one with you. You have made us one with you. You have taught us that if we are open to one another, You dwell in us. Help us to preserve this openness and to fight for it with all our hearts. Help us to realize that there can be no understanding where there is mutual rejection. . . . Fill us then with your love, and let us be bound together with love as we go about our diverse ways, united in this one spirit which makes you present in the world, and which makes you witness to the ultimate reality that is love. Love has overcome. Love is victorious. Amen.

That prayer was said with no explicit reference to Christ nor was it said "in the name of Christ." Does that mean, as some allege either approvingly or disapprovingly, that Merton had, at this stage in his life, "transcended" or "moved beyond" Christianity into a more universalistic religious realm in which specific doctrinal forms of spirituality had been relativized?

What needs to be said, at the outset, is something that stands as a first principle. This is a prayer by a person who was, by self-definition, a Christian monk who belonged to the Christian community. As a consequence of this irreducible fact, when he prayed, he prayed as a Christian. To say it another way: Any prayer by a Christian invokes Jesus and prays with him by the very fact that the prayer is made regardless of the words of the prayer. Only the extreme case of a prayer that denied Christ *ex professo* is "outside of Christ." Prayer and pray-er cannot be seen as abstractions free from the culture within which a person stands. On that point I am in agreement with those who insist that unmediated experiences are chimeras of the philosophical mind. That philosophical truth holds for experience generally and the spiritual life in particular.

Secondly, not only is Merton's prayer saturated with sentiments that are both scriptural and traditional, but also one goes further and notes that the sentiments of the prayer are not only consonant with the sentiments of the *Abba* experience but are also centered on them. Hence, prayer is to be judged by the degree to which it articulates a sense of the gracious relationship that exists between pray-er and God. In that sense, without any spirit of religious imperialism, prayers, from whatever source, may well be appropriated by the Christian community. Such enrichments of our spiritual heritage are quite consonant with the Second Vatican Council's insistence that the Christian community rejects nothing which is "true and holy" in other religious traditions (see *Nostra Aetate*, art. 2). To pray in that fashion is, bluntly, to pray with Jesus.

Without pressing this issue too far we can cite one more, rather traditional, example. Here is one of the oldest prayers in honor of the Blessed Virgin Mary, datable, if one accepts the conclusions of certain scholars, to the end of the third century:

> Under your mercy, we take refuge, Mother of God, do not reject our supplications in necessity. But deliver us from danger. [You] alone chaste; [you] alone blessed. Amen.

That prayer, in its later Latin form known as the *Sub Tuum Praesidium*, comes to us from an ancient Greek papyrus. What is startling about it is that, in this ancient form, it addresses the Virgin without reference to God or Christ in a direct manner. Detached from any context (the prayer may well have been a liturgical one) it seems to reflect a common objection that Mary is seen apart from a christological context and hence denigrates the unique mediatorship of Jesus as Lord.

I said "detached from any context" because the point to be pressed is this: All prayer in the Catholic tradition is uttered "in Christ." To say it another way: It would be impossible to turn to Mary in prayer without recalling that Mary has significance only in the context of Christology. That point is insisted upon not to argue polemically against those who resist Marian devotions but to press the far more fundamental proposition that all prayer in the Catholic tradition assumes, explicitly or tacitly, that when we pray, we pray in union with Christ. Prayers to the Blessed Mother and/or the saints makes sense only in the context of Christology and, by extension, of the doctrine of the communion of the saints. Detached from those truths the very invocation of the saints is a deformation.

When the Second Vatican Council pointed out that there was a hierarchy of truths in Catholicism, it did so not to say that certain truths were less important than others but to show that doctrine in Christianity must be viewed holistically—as part of a whole. At the center of this web of doctrinal formulations, however, is the root truth that God is revealed to us in Jesus who is called the Christ. To skew that basic formulation is to poison all that the church stands for. By analogy, we can say that as Catholic Christians all our prayer is valid when it is consonant with that same truth, attests it, and adds to it.

There is a further point to be pressed. It is that we must resist the temptation to be overly fundamentalistic in our approach to prayer after the manner of Christ. It does not do justice to the inexhaustible mysteries of the Gospel to say that by imitating a "picture" of how Christ prayed suffices for every and all Christians. We simply cannot translate a naïve image of the Gospel into our lives and say that this is prayer after the manner of Jesus, or that that is the way one must pray in imitation of Christ. As we have already indicated, the Catholic tradition has fastened on many aspects of the Gospel portraits of Christ to develop variegated strategies of prayer.

Positively speaking, we must insist that in the person of Jesus there is a "surplus of meaning" upon which the person of prayer may draw. At one level, this surplus of meaning comes from the various styles of prayer that one can intuit from the Gospels: the solitary prayer of Jesus in the desert, the communal experience of Jesus at prayer in the company of his disciples, the prayers of exorcisms and healings, the prayer of praise in the Johannine corpus, and so on. The very variety of those "prayer situations" lends warrant to the same variety of prayer experiences in the Christian tradition.

At a deeper level there is the radical demystification of prayer that Jesus presents both through injunction and through example. The usual patterns of prayer are—to borrow a much-abused word—decentered and deconstructed so that authentic prayer comes from unexpected persons and under quite improbable circumstances. Thus Jesus thanks God for hiding his truth from "the wise and understanding and revealing them to babes" (see Luke 10:21–22), just as he excoriates those who, in the words of Isaiah, praise God with words but reject him in their hearts (see Mark 7:6–7). Furthermore, in a famous passage in Matthew (6:5–8), Jesus both insists on the integrity of prayer by contrasting genuine prayer with that of the "hypocrites" who use prayer for social standing ("they love to stand . . . that they might be seen by men") and by contrasting true prayer with the quasi-magical incantations (the heaping up of empty phrases) of the pagans.

Even more compelling are the exemplars of genuine prayer who are described and praised in the Gospels. The God-fearing centurion (Luke 7:1–10) is lauded for a faith that accepts the power of Jesus to heal without demanding his presence: "Lord, I am not worthy to have you come under my roof . . . but say the word and let my servant be healed." Jesus, Luke crisply records, "marveled at him." In that same Gospel (Luke 7:36–50) Jesus praises the generous impulse of the woman who anoints his feet despite the protestations of the Pharisees who judge her to be a sinner. The calculus of Jesus is simple: She is forgiven much for she has loved much. Her instincts, in short, have come from a sense of genuine relationship and deep existential trust; she goes in peace because, as Jesus says, her faith has saved her.

It is easy, but mistaken, to see in these and similar passages a rejection of the public prayer of Judaism in the name of a higher, more prophetically driven relationship with God. The rest of the Gospel allows no such conclusion. Jesus was punctilious in his liturgical and social-religious obligations with respect to the worship of the temple, the attendance at synagogues, and the rituals of the home. What is clear, however, is that these social manifestations of Jesus' prayer life are authentically connected to his sense of *Abba*. Furthermore, he sees in the instinctive impulses of people toward him a genuinely deep faith. Neither the centurion nor the woman was regularized vis-à-vis the religious matrix of their society. They were, to that extent, outsiders. Yet their prayers are lauded because of their authenticity. What these texts demonstrate, in short, is a continual process of refinement of the very notion of what constitutes genuine prayer.

Nowhere is the authenticity of prayer better described than in the parable of the Pharisee and the publican (tax collector). The story, typically, is in Luke (18:9–14), which is a treasure house of prayer exemplars. We should first note that the setting of the parable is the temple at Jerusalem. The prayer setting is one of traditional devotionalism. Secondly, as is obvious, the polarization is of "types," that is, the seemingly pious Pharisee and the apparently impious tax collector. Thirdly, as the conclusion makes clear, it is the tax collector who went down to his house "justified," and not the Pharisee. Why? The answer is to be found by inquiring into the object of the two pray-ers to which, like spectators at a play, we are privy. Both speak about themselves, but the publican, unlike the Pharisee, speaks about himself *in relation to God*. The Pharisee is condemned not because of who he is but because he speaks only of himself even in the presence of God. The publican's prayer does not even invoke the repeated "I" of the Pharisee. His prayer is in the passive, the passive of dependence: "God, be merciful to me a sinner." It might be noted that Luke calls the publican "justified"—the only time in the Gospels that such a word is used of an individual.

The key to understanding Luke's parable, then, is in the nature of the relationship that it illumines. The publican is justified because he recognizes an Other in his prayer to whom he owes his right to pray. The point, of course, is not that all prayer must be a profession of guilt. The point is that no prayer can be authentic if it does not reach beyond the self to God. That is what the life of Jesus is writ large. What the publican tell us is that he is not an autonomous person. Both men signify nonautonomy by presenting themselves at the temple, but only the publican is able to articulate that dependency through his gestures (always the gestures!) and his words. The circle of the Pharisee bends back to himself; the circle of the publican arcs up from himself to God. Furthermore, and finally, we should note that the publican prays authentically (and the Pharisee inauthentically) *in the temple*. The force of the story derives from a sense of authentication and not from some putative tension between temple prayer and prayer outside the temple.

Like the fictional man who walks out of his house, takes a turn, wanders around the world, and finds himself once again at his home, those who search the Gospels to ask about prayer come back always to the figure of Jesus. As Christians we can say, in the Spirit, that Jesus is Lord and that is adoration enough. Jesus, the first-born of every creature, is also the person who teaches us, beyond words, how to pray. His life is his teaching. And his life teaches us that, first of all, he prayed with absolute simplicity and absolute conviction: *Abba*, Father. He is the preeminent Pray-er. Jesus as Pray-er is never depicted as detached from the community from which he came. He prayed as a Jew in a Jewish setting.

Secondly, the Gospels tell us that many prayed to him in his lifetime for forgiveness, healing, and instruction. Those prayers have been given to us not as an archive but as an encouragement for us to do the same. Thus, the Gospels give us not only the prayer of Jesus as a model, but also many models of those who prayed to and with Jesus. The Gospels testify to the belief of the Christian communities who wrote them that one can address Jesus as Lord and that he responds to that invocation.

Thirdly, Jesus singles out powerful examples of authentic prayer and those examples, more often than not, come from people at the edges and/or on the margins: penitent sinners, socially marginal people, pagan soldiers, repentant felons. In all those cases, prayer comes directly from the heart and is always heard. The fundamental lesson of those exemplars is that all authentic prayer comes, not from a social situation or privileged status, but from the hearts of those who, like Jesus, are confident of the *Abba* who both brings us into being and, nourishes us on our life's journey. That is why he has taught us to dare to say "our Father."

Finally, the prayer of Jesus was nourished on and rooted in the piety of biblical Judaism. Jesus does not resist the praise of the Psalms or the images of the great pray-ers of his past. He absorbed them in his person, and that absorption made him who he was. His language was the biblical language that he inherited and made his own. We insist on that point because it reinforces a thesis basic to this chapter: When we pray, for example, the Psalms, we pray them with Jesus (who also prayed them) and through Jesus to the God whom he called *Abba*.

A Prayer

Lord Jesus, we pray thy mercy on our table spread,
And what thy gentle hands have given thy men
Let it by thee be blessed; whate'er we have
Came from thy lavish heart and gentle hand,
And all that's good is thine, for thou art good.
And ye that eat, give thanks for it to Christ,
And let the words ye utter be only peace,
For Christ loved peace: it was himself who said,
Peace, I give to you, my peace I leave with you.
Grant that our own may be a generous hand
Breaking the bread for all poor men, sharing the food.
Christ shall receive the bread thou gavest his poor,
And shall not tarry to give thee reward. Amen.

This prayer, in a fine translation by the late Helen Waddell, was written as a Latin lyric by Alcuin of York (735–804). Alcuin, more than any other single person, was the fountainhead of those educational, liturgical, and religious reforms at the court of Charlemagne that now bear the name of the Carolingian Renaissance. He composed educational treatises, reformed liturgical books, and produced an edition of Jerome's Vulgate.

While not a monk himself, he was deeply influenced by monastic spirituality and saturated in biblical, patristic, and liturgical literature. To that extensive theological background, Alcuin brought a profound knowledge of Latin literature (he lamented his Vergilian passion in old age) which allowed him to express his piety in fine Latin.

What is most admirable about this deeply christological prayer is its compression of a number of basic themes into a unified whole. Beginning with sentiments of thanksgiving for the food provided through the providence of God, Alcuin quickly expresses such beneficence *in nomine Christi* in terms that are both eucharistic (Eucharist-thanksgiving) and communal. The final coda of the prayer is enormously suggestive where we ask Christ to give us a generous hand as we break bread "for all poor men." In that succinct final supplication we recall Christ in the ordinary activity of life, in the representation of him in the Eucharist and in the lives of the poor while hoping for that "reward" which is, as the scriptures tell us, eternal life.

A Note on Readings

My research for this chapter started with a notebook in which I wrote out (the discipline is a fine one!) all of the texts in which Jesus speaks directly on prayer. I was aided in my understanding of the prayer(s) of Jesus by the following books: James P. Mackey's *Jesus the Man and the Myth* (Ramsey, NJ: Paulist, 1979), Walter Kasper's *Jesus the Christ* (Ramsey, NJ: Paulist, 1977), and William M. Thompson's *The Jesus Debate: A Survey and Synthesis* (Ramsey, NJ: Paulist, 1985). These books are all indebted to the classic study of Joachim Jeremias: *The Prayers of Jesus* (Philadelphia: Fortress, 1967). On the primitive eucharistic community I relied on Wayne Meeks's *The First Urban Christians: The Social World of the Apostle Paul* (New Haven, CN: Yale University Press, 1983). Jon Sobrino's *Christology at the Crossroads* (Maryknoll, NY: Orbis, 1978) has a searching chapter on the prayer of Jesus from a liberationist perspective. I have also learned much from Robert Krieg's *Story-Shaped Christology: The Role of Narratives in Identifying Jesus Christ* (Mahwah, NJ: Paulist, 1988).

On the centrality of prayer in Luke, see A. Trites, "The Prayer Motif in Luke-Acts," in *Perspectives on Luke-Acts*, edited by Charles H. Talbert (Danville, VA: Association of Baptist Professors of Religion, 1978), pp. 168–86.

On Ruusbroec's writings, see *John Ruusbroec: The Spiritual Espousals and Other Writings*, an excellent edition translated by James A. Wiseman, O.S.B. (Mahwah, NJ: Paulist, 1985). Harvey Egan's *Christian Mysticism: The Future of a Tradition* (New York: Pueblo, 1984) was very helpful for its pages on Christ mysticism.

Rahner's notion of the Concrete Absolute is discussed succinctly in *The Practice of Faith: A Handbook of Contemporary Spirituality* (New York: Crossroad, 1983), p. 136–41.

Thomas Merton's essay "The Humanity of Christ in Monastic Prayer" can be found in *The Monastic Journey*, edited by Patrick Hart (Garden City, NY: Doubleday Image, 1978), pp. 121–44. I also found useful the essay "Christ in the Contemplative Tradition," in Noel Dermot O'Donoghue's *The Holy Mountain: Approaches to the Mystery of Prayer* (Wilmington, DL: Glazier, 1983), pp. 18–32. George Kilcourse's essay "The Horizon of Thomas Merton's Christology," *Cistercian Studies* 23 (1988), pp. 169–89, is a fine survey.

The notion of *coincidentia oppositorum* is treated with great sensitivity in Ewert Cousins's *Bonaventure and the Coincidence of Opposites* (Chicago: Franciscan Herald, 1978). I have also benefitted from an unpublished paper of Professor Cousins entitled "Bonaventure and Dante: The Role of Christ in the Spiritual Journey."

Harvey Egan's *Christian Mysticism: The Future of a Tradition* (New York: Pueblo, 1984) has fine pages on Christ-centered prayer in the mystical tradition. Sebastian Moore's *The Crucified Jesus Is No Stranger* (New York: Seabury, 1977) is centrally concerned with the person of Jesus Christ in the life of prayer.

Christian Spirituality: Origins to the Twelfth Century, edited by Bernard McGinn et al., has three essays germane to our topic: John Meyendorff's "Christ as Savior in the East," pp. 231–52; Bernard McGinn's "Christ as Savior in the West,"

pp. 253–59; Leonid Ouspensky's "Icon and Art," pp. 382–94.
All have ample bibliographies.

For the dating and significance of the *Sub Tuum Praesidium*, see the entry *sub voce* in *Theotokos: A Theological Encyclopedia of the Blessed Virgin Mary*, edited by Michael O'Carroll (Wilmington, DL: Glazier, 1986).

6

EUCHARIST

*The bread which is transcendent is
the same thing as the name of God.*

Simone Weil

We have called upon the liturgy so often in the course of
this book that it would be unthinkable not to dwell on the
heart of the liturgy, which is the celebration of the Eucharist.
The Eucharist, after all, is the natural complement of the proclaimed Word in the liturgy, and both Word and Eucharist are
the energy source for the community which is church: "And
they devoted themselves to the apostles' teaching and fellowship, to the breaking of bread and prayers" (Acts 2:42).

Any discussion of the Eucharist today inevitably brings
with it certain very different challenges precisely because we
are now in a period of the church's life in which a profound
shift has taken place with respect to the Eucharist. That shift,
brought about in and immediately after the great events of
the Second Vatican Council, can be described briefly as a
shift from a certain kind of *presence* to a new understanding
of that term. Only Catholics of a certain age (and they are
rapidly aging!) can existentially appreciate the distance of that
shift. When we speak of *presence* here we have less in mind
theological disputes about the doctrine of transubstantiation
or transignification but rather the sense one has that the celebration of the real presence of Christ is perceived more today
in the celebration of the Eucharist than in the reserved presence of Christ in the Eucharist. That shift does not imply the

denial of one thing and the affirmation of another, but it does clearly underscore a shift in emphasis.

A brief autobiographical note (not too drenched in nostalgia, one hopes) may make the point. Most Catholics of my age can dredge up from old family albums First Communion pictures that are very similar to my own: a slightly pious-looking lad of seven dressed in preposterous white knickers with a white jacket, white shirt and tie, with white long socks and shoes. Clutched in the hands of that ghostly juvenile would be a white-covered prayerbook (with a depressed inner cover in which a fake gold crucifix was glued) and a white rosary cunningly intertwined through the fingers. Girls would be similarly attired in dresses with a while mantilla or veil to boot. We may or may not have also carried a white candle (memory fails me here) for the Big Day.

Thus garbed, on a Sunday in early June, as the second grade-school year drew to a close, we approached the altar (banked in flowers, candles blazing, priestly chasubles stiff with gold thread) to kneel at prie-dieus covered with cloths to receive, for the first time, Jesus in Holy Communion. Do not bite on the hosts, the nuns warned us: tilt your head back and put out your tongues, the curate instructed us; do not touch water or food that morning, our parents reminded us. Welcome, King of Kings, Lord of Lords. Welcome, Prisoner of the Tabernacle.

That ceremony—an authentic *rite of passage*—initiated millions of Catholics into the profound mystery of Jesus Christ as truly present in the Sacrament of the altar. Our memories of First Communion must be seen in tandem with all of those manifestations of Catholic piety (mostly of late medieval or post-Tridentine origin) that emphasized the sacramental presence of Christ in the eucharistic elements. Those manifestations range from the practice of the adoration of the Blessed Sacrament (in some religious houses and convents this was done night and day) to the myriad ceremonies—Corpus Christi processions, Benediction of the Blessed Sacrament, Forty Hours Devotions, Eucharistic Congresses, etc.—that were part and parcel of Catholic piety.

The very shape of liturgical rubrics in the pre-Vatican II church were largely shaped by this keen sense of eucharistic

presence. The sharp split between sanctuary and congregation, reinforced by altar rails and altar gates as well as prohi-
bitions against entering that sanctuary and the rubrics for
handling sacred vessels, conspired with the prominence of the
tabernacle (to the detriment of both altar, and still more, the
pulpit) as the focus of attention all tended to say, symboli-
cally, that Who was there, rather than what was happening,
was paramount. There was a very real feeling that Christ was
present as if in a sacred precinct with a courtly cast(e) (of
priests and clergy) attending to this presence who stood afar
from the ordinary faithful. Women entered those precincts to
get married or to make a religious profession or, more typically, to clean and arrange flowers. Period.

This understanding of the Eucharist developed over a long
period of time and, make no mistake about it, there *was* a
development, as any close look at church floor plans in the
West makes clear. This emphasis on the true presence of
Christ was also hastened to the degree that the Reformers re-
interpreted or mitigated the consequences of the doctrine. It
is no accident that religious orders of men and women devoted primarily to the worship of Christ eucharistically
present are, almost without exception, of post-Tridentine origin, even if their roots can be traced back to the medieval period that saw the flowering of things like the Feast of Corpus
Christi, itself of late medieval origin.

The doctrine of the Real Presence has behind it an extremely long and complex development of both doctrinal understandings and liturgical and canonical usages. Nathan
Mitchell's *Cult and Controversy: The Worship of the Eucharist Outside of Mass* tracks a whole series of issues connected
with this development. There was the general erosion of the
right of laypeople to take Communion to the sick and absent;
the slow disappearance of the custom of taking Communion
home after the liturgy; the emergence of the custom of "vis-
iting" the church with its reserved sacrament beginning in
the tenth century, which then expanded into regular visits,
processions, exposition, and benediction with the elements;
the decline of reception of the Sacrament in favor of what
Mitchell calls "ocular communion." One telling fact about
this very complex development is that the custom of putting

the tabernacle on the main altar did not become common (or even permissible) until the sixteenth century. To this day—and it is not an atypical arrangement for cathedral and/or basilica churches—the Eucharist is reserved not on the main altar but in a separate chapel in Saint Peter's in the Vatican. That arrangement is not in any fashion atypical of arrangements in the other ancient Roman basilicas.

To say that there was a development is not to say that the development was an inauthentic or wrongheaded one. While it is true that some eucharistic devotion was sentimentally literal (e.g., Jesus, the Prisoner of the Tabernacle), the plain fact of the matter is that a spirituality focused on the real presence of Christ was a deep source of impressive spiritual resources in the church. That sense of sacramental presence produced a tradition of spiritual poetry (e.g., the offices/hymns of Corpus Christi), a wealth of paraliturgical devotions, and a profound impulse for the life of prayer in extraordinary modern figures ranging from Charles de Foucauld in the last century to the late Thomas Merton in our own time.

For better or worse, there has been a shift, as I noted at the beginning of this chapter, away from that strong focus on the real presence of Christ as it was developed in the late medieval and post-Reformation era. This shift is palpable. We see evidence of it everywhere in the contemporary church. It is reflected in the decline of popular devotions like Benediction of the Blessed Sacrament, just as it is reflected in the architecture of our churches with the new emphasis on pulpit and altar and the "sidelining" of the tabernacle away from its once central place of honor. Nowhere is that shift more clear than in the changes that have taken place in the liturgy itself with its profound shift in rubrics, the emergence of lay ministers of the Eucharist, the pressures for a different model of priesthood, and a vernacular, participation-based liturgy. Most significantly of all, there has been less of a focus on the liturgy as the instrument by which the presence of Christ is effected to an emphasis on the very celebration of this mystery.

This profound change, less than a full generation old, has not been without deep pain and disappointment for many people. One frequent lament is that the "mystery" and "sa-

credness" have disappeared from the liturgy. More militant
critics of this shift have noisily protested that what we have
seen in the space of twenty-five years is the "protestantiza-
tion" of the Roman Catholic liturgy in general and the loss
of that deep respect Catholics once held for the Eucharist in
particular. "It is bitterly hard for someone with an unrecon-
structed Catholic heart to bear," writes Anne Roche Mug-
geridge, "that the glorious universal prayer of all the Catholic
ages [she refers to the Mass] in which, whatever his race or
station, he unselfconsciously used to join, has been remain-
dered into a barely tolerated cultural survival."

Change has, in fact, taken place, and the question before us
is to understand the ramifications of that change for the life
of prayer. In the first place, we will simply state that the shift
has taken place and the consequence of it is that we now have
a clearer conception of the Eucharist as a communal celebration as distinct from the devotion that devolves from the sacramental presence of Christ in the Eucharist. In a sense what
has happened is that the contemporary Catholic church has
not become more Protestant but more in line, *mutatis
mutandis*, with the Eastern Christian emphasis on the liturgy
as the place and time *par excellence* where we meet the living, real, sacramental, and glorified Christ.

We shall begin, then, with the observation that it is in the
celebration of the Eucharist that we meet, pray with, give adoration to, and express our hope in, the person of Jesus Christ.
To be a simple undifferentiated believer may rest on an affirmation of Christ, but to be a Catholic Christian is to celebrate Christ in a quite specific manner. The Second Vatican
Council put the matter apodictically when it said that there
is no true Christian community unless "it has as its basis
and center the celebration of the most Holy Eucharist" (*Decree on the Life and Ministry of Priests*, art. 6).

What does that mean in the concrete? I shall put the matter
in a series of extended propositions.

In the first place, when a community (of whatever size or
makeup) gathers for the celebration of the Eucharist, the one
central fact of the gathering is that the community meets to
re-present, re-create, re-enact, and re-member the living, res-

urrected Christ who gave us this celebration "in memory of him" to be celebrated "until he comes again" (see 1 Cor. 11:23–26). I have hyphenated the verbs in the preceding statement for the precise reason of underscoring the Eucharist as a dynamic reality in which a believing community joins with the priest in doing something as a community that has a model or paradigm in the very acts and instructions of the Lord. The Eucharist is not something external to the worship of believers out there as an object (even an object of adoration), but an act in which Jesus Christ becomes truly present in the Communion species and in a heightened manner in the believing worship of the community.

It is my very deep conviction that if we do not start with that act of worship, within which we identify with Christ who is made present in his salvific power, our understanding of the Eucharist in the life of prayer is in real danger of being skewed. Never is our prayer more authentically Christian than when we gather around the altar to participate in those mysteries. For it is in those moments when we really and authentically join with Christ in common worship.

The communal nature of this primordial act of worship needs to be underscored because it is there that the fullest sense of catholicity is present. The Catholic concept of faith is not a vertical model in which there is myself and God to the exclusion of the community, in the sense that we are called into the New Covenant whose pledge is Christ. In fact, as the unbroken testimony of the church's witness testifies, every small community (e.g., a parish) is a microcosm (the *ecclesiola*) of the whole bond of believers whom we call the Communion of Saints. There is, in short, no genuine Catholic life of prayer unless it is rooted in the gathered celebration of the mysteries of Jesus Christ in the liturgy. The statement of faith set out by the World Council of Churches in Lima (1982) put the matter nicely: The Eucharist signifies what the world is to become.

The lessons to be drawn from the centrality of the liturgy for the spiritual life of Catholics are many. In the first place, this fact should act as a spur to everyone to be concerned with the quality of the liturgy. Secondly, it is a warning to those who attempt to fashion a spirituality apart from the liturgical life of the church. It is, likewise, a salutary warning to those who grouse about the horizontal (i.e., communal) nature of the reformed liturgy since, at its heart, liturgy is communally horizontal with a vertically transcendental element to it. Finally, since the liturgy derives from our experience as human beings in community we should expect that such a sense of community is always going to be subject to the vagaries of human failure.

There is in the celebration of the Eucharist a kind of tension and polarity that extends in a number of directions. We are admonished to come to the Eucharist in a spirit of faith and contrition, but it is the very essence of the dynamics of the Eucharist that strengthens faith and nourishes a need for conversion. The Eucharist demands of us a spirit of unity, but it is the Eucharist which guarantees that unity. We are called upon to share in the Eucharist as a body of believers, but the Eucharist is also, and simultaneously, the most transcendentally personal religious act in which the individual participates. The Eucharist, at the same time, re-calls the memory of Christ, makes him present in the here and now, and points to the final time when we will no longer need the Eucharist. The Eucharist, according to the traditional Catholic understanding, re-presents the sacrifice of Christ on the cross which was, also, a once-and-forever event in the story of salvation. It is not mere rhetoric that allows the church to call the Eucharist, *par excellence*, the *Mysterium Fidei*—the great mystery of faith.

From the earliest beginnings of the church's life it was customary to carry the Eucharist away from the church gathering to give to those who, for one reason or another, could not attend the liturgy. There is ample evidence that the custom of reserving the Eucharist in private homes (as well as in the churches) was an early Christian practice. From that datum two facts may be plausibly deduced: One is that the early church did not reserve the notion of the sacramental presence of Christ to the actual performance of the liturgy and, secondly, the church, in its earliest days, saw an intimate connection between the celebration of the liturgy and the extended lives of the community. Both of those facts need some reflection. We will begin with the latter observation first.

At its most elementary level, the reservation of the Eucharist signifies that the celebration of the liturgy is not detached from the ordinary life of the church. The community that worships has an obligation to the sick and absent who are not there at the celebration. That is a shorthand way of observing that the liturgy radiates out to the larger life of the church. Again, this is something that we need to affirm as we come to the liturgy, as well as something that the liturgy teaches us in our celebration. The Eucharist is there for all. It is not a flight or rhetorical fancy to say that the reservation of the Sacrament is a sign that there are those who do not communicate but who belong at the altar. It is not merely a question of the sick. When we see a tabernacle we must learn that the living Christ is there for the alienated, the divorced, the indifferent, the despairing, the faltering believer, and all those who have a rightful call to celebrate the mysteries of Christ. It is not simply a flourish of language when we describe a person returning to the practice of the faith as one who "comes back to the sacraments," just as we—on rare occasions—refuse the Sacrament (excommunication) to those who egregiously violate Christian decency and its moral imperatives.

There is, then, a fundamental ethical dimension to the Eucharist that is reflected both in its celebration and in the continuing presence of Christ when the celebration is finished. When we begin to plumb that fact there is a vast arena for self-criticism and self-chastisement. When we think of Christ truly present in the Eucharist we should think of those who are not present but who have a right to be there: the sick, the impoverished, the lost souls of our streets, the neglected, as well as those legions of people who are not respectable. On many occasions I have wandered into large urban churches at odd hours to see a range of humanity from drunks sleeping off cheap port or the mentally afflicted mumbling to themselves, to business people and kids playing or sitting or wandering around the aisles. And I have said, "Yes. Quite right. They all belong here and Christ welcomes them no matter how off-putting I, in my narrow fastidiousness, may find them."

Still and all, it is useful to recall that the presence of Christ
in the Eucharist should not be thought of in any exclusive or
absolute manner. The 1967 Vatican *Instruction on Eucharistic Worship* wisely notes that Christ is present sacramentally
in the church in a number of ways. Christ is present in the
assembly gathered in his name. He is present in the Word
preached and proclaimed. He is present in the one who presides. Finally, Christ is present in the Eucharist and that presence is called "real not in an exlusive sense, as if other kinds
of presence were not real, but *par excellence.*" What the
church teaches, in short, is that Christ is sacramentally
present in a very dense and pluriform manner, with the Eucharist being the apex of that presence. We need to absorb the
lesson of that *instruction* because we impoverish the living
presence of Christ in the church if we focus solely on his eucharistic presence, however preeminent that presence is in
the Catholic tradition.

That sense of the continuing presence of the sacramental
Christ is not only palpable for the local church. It is the constant teaching of the church that in the celebration of Christ
we, to borrow an adage from ecology, "act locally but think
globally." That is a way of describing the bond which links
the local community with the great church and the present
with the past and those yet to come. That notion of unity has
been described in the prayer of the *Didache* in words that still
ring true:

> As this broken bread was scattered over the mountains and
> when brought together becomes one, so let your church be
> brought together from the ends of the earth into your king-
> dom; for yours are the glory and the power through Jesus
> Christ for evermore.

This sense of community is also intensified by asking, as
the Anglican theologian Kenneth Leech suggests, where does
the grain and the grapes come from that we use at the liturgy? Who provides us with the gifts of the altar? What obligations do we owe them? How do they participate in our
celebrations? It is very much a helpful sign, I think, that at

recent Eucharistic Congresses (like that of 1976), which can have an air of baroque triumphalism to them, there were addresses by figures like Mother Teresa and Dom Helder Camara on the need to link the Eucharist to the needs of the hungry and destitute of the world. This is a topic of such importance that we will reiterate it further when we consider the "political" dimensions of prayer.

How then does our eucharistic prayer become Catholic prayer? Fundamentally, the terms are interchangeable. Descriptively, eucharistic prayer is Catholic prayer when we learn to celebrate the real presence of Christ in the Eucharist as our Lord and Savior while affirming our unity with the entire church, symbolized by our Communion at the liturgy and our will to unite ourselves with, in the words of the liturgy, "our absent brethren." That prayer is all the more authentic when we have a lively sense that the real presence of Christ extends beyond the liturgy to those who cannot or do not come to the altar. Eucharistic prayer is, in short, immanent (we find Christ in the community of belief), transcendental (we celebrate the risen Christ), and ethically political (we are called to give thanks with all those who do not or cannot share in the celebration that we take for granted). Finally, we need to remind ourselves that it is in *nourishment* that the Eucharist finds its deepest meaning. The early church permitted home reservation not primarily for adoration but as Communion for "the absent brethren."

Eucharistic prayer is the deep center and firm matrix from which all other Catholic prayer arises. That is the firm conviction of this book and, I think, the unswerving teaching of the church. Nonetheless, there is a lamentable tendency to see the life of contemplative prayer as something quite different from the liturgical life. One need only look at the plethora of books on spirituality to see how little attention is paid to the liturgy in general and the Eucharist in particular when contemplative prayer is discussed. The recent trends in spirituality (no matter how fruitful they may be) have a tendency to emphasize meditative or prayer techniques at the expense of the very heart of Catholic prayer which is the liturgy.

In the chapter on reading I suggested one technique of linking ordinary daily prayer to the scriptural proclamations of the church. Here I would like to focus more on the connection of liturgy and contemplation in general with some specific reference(s) to the Eucharist. This is an enormously complicated subject that has generated a vast literature over the years. The main lines of the issue seem to be these: How does one reconcile the seemingly personal and private drive for prayer with the basic need to celebrate the liturgy in common as part of a believing community? If one wishes to use images: What links the figure of Christ alone on the mountaintop praying to the Father and the Christ of the Last Supper? How do we tie together those models of prayer that the New Testament provides for us?

That there is a problem was noticed more than a generation ago by Hans Urs von Balthasar in his classic book *Prayer*. Von Balthasar noted that many people find the language of the liturgy too arcane, too stylized, and too rapid (he was thinking of the Latin liturgy) to nourish many people. The fact that the liturgy did not go at one's own pace created problems for the cultivation of prayer. Furthermore, the liturgy does not seem to provide that private space which many people need for prayer. Yet, there is the irreducible fact that the liturgy is prayer *par excellence*. How does one fill the gap between these two styles of prayer?

The obvious, but not very satisfactory, answer is that one can pray alone as an individual and as a member of a community. I say "not very satisfactory" because the essential heart of Catholic prayer is the Eucharist and the question perdures: How link that prayer with our need for solitary prayer if we want the latter to be authentically and fully Catholic? To put the matter another way: We can pray individually with great integrity, but we can pray as Catholics only by participation in the liturgy and, further, that basic prayer needs to involve all other prayer. From that general principle we may adduce some links between eucharistic prayer and private prayer which might help bridge the difficulties of keeping both in tandem.

In the first place, the liturgy reminds us of a salutary truth: Our faith is rooted in material realities, which is to say, our faith is incarnational. Participation in the liturgy not only helps us to keep in check any contemplative flights not rooted in God's revelation, but it also acts as a source of nourishment for our prayer through our encounter with both Word and Sacrament.

Just as participation in the liturgy keeps us close to the sacramental and incarnational realities of our faith, it also forcefully shields us from any excessive privatization of faith. Our life of prayer should never degenerate into a program of self-scrutiny and self-therapy. Prayer is prayer in the church and with the church. More significantly, it is prayer *with Christ*. That prayer is most perfectly realized in the liturgy, and its realization should resonate beyond the actual time we spend in church.

Secondly, the liturgy helps to *remind* us of the saving works of Christ. It is of the essence of the liturgy to be a memorial, a remembrance. It is not accidental that the great eucharistic prayers of the liturgy begin with words that emphasize this function: "In memory of his death and resurrection" (Eucharistic Prayer II); "Father, calling to mind the death your Son endured for us" (Eucharistic Prayer III); "We now celebrate this memorial of our redemption" (Eucharistic Prayer IV); "We do this in memory of Jesus Christ" (Eucharistic Prayer for Mass of Reconciliation I), etc.

By our insertion into the ongoing liturgical life of the church we testify to the great things of Christ by recalling them to mind and making them present in our place and time. That act of religious memory stands as a fountain for all other prayer. It makes us recall why we pray, with whom, for what ends, and to whom. It is possible to pray in a generic fashion (think of the "neutral" prayers composed by those who want such activities in public schools!) but one can enter into the liturgical prayer of the church only as a follower of Christ. The liturgy in general and the Eucharist in particular are irreducibly christocentric. It is precisely for that reason that Karl Rahner can write (as he did in *Foundations of Christian Faith*) that one cannot speak of the Eucharist as one of the seven sacraments in a simple fashion. The Eucharist is, above all, the church's Sacrament because, in Rahner's words, "it is precisely the institution of the Lord's Supper which is of decisive importance for the founding of the church and for the self-understanding of Jesus Christ as the mediator of salvation." The Eucharist, then, is the sacrament of ecclesiality precisely because it is the great reminder of what we are, why we exist as a church, and what stands at the church's center.

To summarize: The Eucharist, at the very heart of the Catholic reality, is sacramental, incarnational, and the vehicle of making present the living Christ in time and space. It is from those characteristics as we encounter them in our faith experience of the living Christ that should (or better, must) shape and energize all of our other prayer. As we privately pray in adoration, thanksgiving, penitence, or petition we do so in our own words and according to our own impulses. Nonetheless, overarching those private moments with God there is the deeply real presence of Christ, encountered in the Eucharist, that keeps us within the mind and intentions of Christ. It is from that center that all prayer should radiate.

Because of the centrality of the eucharistic liturgy the postconciliar tendency to allow for the liturgy to be celebrated in less-formal settings for special occasions is to be applauded. The notion of home Masses, small liturgies, etc., helps to bring people to a greater focus on what is essential and crucial for the faith. Such an emphasis also brings with it grave responsibilities in the church to value the liturgy and to afford it the central place it deserves in the life of the church. Indeed, if one wants a rule of thumb to judge a parish that is "working," a simple empirical test can be administered: Does that parish have a dignified, well-thought-out, and serious liturgy?

It is also important to dwell on this fact because it stands behind many seemingly disparate debates in the church about ministry and so on. The root issue is always: How well does the church provide for the celebration of the Eucharist? All questions of tradition (with a small "t") must be seen in the light of the needs of the great Tradition of the liturgy.

What of extraliturgical eucharistic devotions?

A good deal of such piety derives from the thirteenth century when, because of earlier doctrinal disputes, people's attention began to move from the action of the liturgy to the real presence of Christ in the eucharistic elements and the "moment" when this transformation took place. One can trace, though it is hardly a straight line, an evolution taking place that begins with a focus on the elevation of the host and chalice at Mass to dwell on those elements that created the Feast of Corpus Christi, the practice of eucharistic processions in tandem with the feast, and the emergence of blessings with the consecrated elements (i.e., Benediction of the Blessed Sacrament), and an increased emphasis on the tabernacle rather than on the altar. Indeed, one can see in many churches (especially late medieval and post-Tridentine churches in Europe) the entire focus of the architecture on the tabernacle with the altar nearly reduced to a supporting table to hold its presence. The basic thing to keep in mind is that these devotional practices and emphases are relatively late, and historically conditioned, realities in the life of the church.

However much this shift may have contributed to an increase in piety, one should note that such a shift carried with it the seeds of abuse and a skewed sense of authentic eucharistic theology. That is hardly a new insight. One can look at the writings of the most representative liturgical scholars of this century (Jungmann, Dix, Bouyer, etc.) to see their criticisms of this kind of piety as it tended to lurch toward sentimentalism and triumphalism. The fact that some of this devotionalism is on the wane today is a direct result of the church's attempt to recover a more authentic, traditional, and scripturally based theology of the Eucharist.

That being said, we can still affirm that the constant practice of the church in reserving the Eucharist in our churches attests to the church's belief in the continuing real presence of Christ in the sacrament. One sees, for instance, in the 1983 *Code of Canon Law* (especially canons 934–44) legislation designed to encourage adoration of Christ in the Eucharist outside the liturgy. In fact, canon 937 specifically orders churches to be open for a certain number of hours so that the faithful can "spend time in prayer before the Most Blessed Sacrament." Canon 938 orders the tabernacle to be placed in some part of the church where it will be conspicuous and suitable for prayer. Canon 940 orders a sanctuary lamp to be kept lit to signify the presence of the Blessed Sacrament in the church.

Our post-conciliar emphasis on liturgy should not blind us to the fitting character of praying before the Blessed Sacrament in the setting of a church. What one can see, upon reflection, is that such devotion carries with it the possibility of enlarging our spiritual sense.

In the first place, to go to church to pray is a primordial religious gesture that provides us with a sense of the reality of the Sacred. To step into a church is to leave the profane world (the word *profane* literally means "outside the temple or sacred place") to enter the world of God. That act, in itself, is an act of piety and an impetus for turning to God in prayer. It is an act or gesture that has its own meaning and, as such, as we have argued in another place in this book, is a gesture of prayer in its own right. At this level we can be straightforwardly apodictic: To pray in church before the Blessed Sacrament is a right thing to do and constitutes, in itself, an act of prayer. To pray before the Blessed Sacrament is, in a real sense, an extension of the liturgy itself.

Beyond an act of prayer, devotion to the Blessed Sacrament is an act of faith. To kneel or stand before the Blessed Sacrament says tacitly that we believe in the sacramental presence of Christ and his guarantee that he will be with (and in) the church until he "comes again." That act of faith carries with it implicit affirmations of the Incarnation as well as convictions about the essential task of the church to make present Christ in time and space. In that act of faith, we give our faith in Christ a specificity and concreteness: Christ is *here* in a real way. Nathan Mitchell has called the reserved species in our churches "living icons of a community's actions." It is a wonderfully apt phrase because it points up both the continuing reality of the presence of Christ among us and the active work of the believing community.

That "hereness"—that location in space, if you will—is not simply to place an object somewhere for adoration. We should recall that the primary reason for eucharistic reservation in the early church was for the succor of those who could not attend the liturgy. Hence, the eucharistic presence of Christ is in no way to be construed as some species of the "Prisoner of the Tabernacle." Christ is sacramentally present in our churches as a sign that the liturgical celebrations of his reality extend beyond the physical confines of the church and, more especially, to those people who are most vulnerable and impeded from active participation in the life of the church.

There seems little doubt that the keen sense of the presence of Christ in the Eucharist as it was once understood is on the wane. There has been, and will continue to be, a diminishment of those devotional practices which emphasize the presence of Christ in that fashion. This fact should not distress those who understand something about the Christian tradition. Such devotionalism came into the church at a specific time in church history in response to certain specific theological and cultural conditions. That devotionalism increased and multiplied over the years often, we should note, at the expense of other understandings of Christ's presence. As Nathan Mitchell has observed, the church underwent a profound shift in the early Middle Ages as it moved away from eating as a form of Communion to what Mitchell calls "ocular communion." It was not until early in this century, with the move toward more frequent Communion, that there was a swing back to the older paradigm. That shift would receive great impetus from the reforms of the Second Vatican Council.

Each age must rediscover ways in which it finds the presence of Christ. Ours has been a time in which that discovery comes easily in the act of celebration and memorialization in the liturgy. Furthermore, as the church has constantly taught us, Christ is truly present in ways other than the sacramental one. Christ is truly present in the proclamation of the scriptures just as he is found in service to the "least" of the brethren.

Our age has found a different (different—not necessarily better) way to sense the real presence of Christ. We affirm Christ as truly present in the Eucharist in the sacramental sense of the term; we affirm his voice in the sacred scriptures of the church; we affirm him in our desire for social justice for those who are not fed their daily bread, much less their heavenly bread. To absorb that search for the real presence of Christ into the actual life of prayer, both private and communal, is the great task of Catholic spirituality in our age.

If anyone should object that the above discussion "waters down" the traditional understanding of the Real Presence as we have received it in the Catholic tradition, we again recall the observations of the Vatican's *Instruction on Eucharistic Worship* (1967), which reflects the teaching of the Second Vatican Council on the liturgy. Christ, the instruction says, is present under the species "not in an exclusive sense, as if other kinds of presence were not real, but *par excellence.*" For the church teaches, and has always taught, that Christ is truly present in assemblies in his name; in his Word preached and proclaimed; in the person who presides at worship; and in the celebration of the Eucharist itself.

The great paradigm of eucharistic devotion can be seen in the story of Jesus on the road to Emmaus. In fact, that story (Luke 24:13–35), redolent with eucharistic symbolism, can be taken as a model for those who wish to pray in the eucharistic mode. On the road to the village of Emmaus two disciples meet Jesus whom they do not recognize. They "explain" to this stranger all the events of Jerusalem and their dashed hopes with the death of Jesus three days previously. The stranger, in turn, "interpreted to them in all the scriptures the things concerning himself" (24:27). The stranger is invited to stay with the two disciples when they arrive at the village. The key verses of the story occur at this point, verses with their echoes of the words of institution of the Eucharist at the Last Supper: "When he was at table with them, he took the bread and blessed it and broke it and gave it to them. And their eyes were opened and they recognized him; and he vanished out of their sight" (24:30–31). Immediately, they knew whom they had seen. They left for Jerusalem to tell the disciples what had happened "on the road and how he was known to them in the breaking of the bread" (24:35).

It is not a flight of fancy to see every believer in the Emmaus disciples. If this story derives from the experiences of the early faith community, its great power comes from the insight that the community had in the way in which Christ was really known. The events of the passion and Resurrection had already taken place. Jesus, not recognized, explains the scriptures to the disciples on the road. It was only at table that they understood who he was and who was with them. This truth is reinforced by Luke when he ends the story by repeating that fact: *He was known to them in the breaking of the bread.* That recognition comes as a kind of narrative peak in the story: Everything leads up to that recognition, and it is recalled for the reader at the very end of the narrative.

The Jesus whom they failed to recognize at first meeting was one whom they had known. What they did not recognize was the now-risen and glorified Lord. In that they were of a kind with those who failed to know Christ when they met him after the Resurrection. The capacity to understand who the risen Lord was occurs precisely when they "break bread."

It is tempting to read this whole story as a kind of scriptural gloss on the transformative power of the liturgy with its celebration of the Word (they said: "Did our hearts not burn within us while he talked to us on the road when he opened to us the scriptures?" [Luke 24:32]) and its revelatory climax in the celebration at table. That event then ends with the apostles going out (in this case, to Jerusalem) to witness to the risen Lord: *Ite, missa est.*

A Prayer

We offer to you, God our Father, Lord of all, an offering and a commemoration and a memorial in the sight of God, living from the beginning and holy from eternity, for the living and the dead, for the near and the far, for the poor and the travelers, for the churches and monasteries which are here and in every place and in all regions; and for me, unworthy and a sinner, whom you have made worthy to stand before you (remember me in your heavenly kingdom!); and for the souls and spirits whom we commemorate before you, Lord, mighty God, and for this people which is in the true faith and awaits your abundant mercy; and for the sins, faults, and defects of us all, we offer this pure and holy offering.

This priestly prayer introduces the eucharistic liturgy of the Maronites, a uniate church centered in Lebanon. Their eucharistic prayer has a close relationship to the so-called Anaphora of Saints Addai and Mari, traceable in part back to the late third century.

Like many of the eucharistic usages of the early church (one thinks immediately of the *Didache*) there is a strong sense of the celebration of the Eucharist as a bond that ties not only the members of the worshiping community but also those who worship in other communities, for the dispossessed and the traveler, for the living and the dead. The community itself is described as already being in the household of the faith but waiting God's "abundant mercy."

The Eucharist is described both as a worshipful offering and as a commemoration/memorial. In a phrase, then, the priest announces an intention both to worship and to preach by the ritual act that is to follow. Like most of these early eucharistic prayers, a whole sacramental theology is compressed into the few words of the formal liturgy. To read those eucharistic prayers is to receive an education in the great christological, ecclesiological, and sacramental themes of the Catholic tradition.

The congregation sets its seal of approval on this petitionary and declamatory prayer by responding, as the rubrics indicate, "It is fitting and right."

This prayer, and many other representative examples, can be found in *Prayers of the Eucharist: Early and Reformed*, edited by R. C. D. Jasper and G. J. Cuming (New York: Oxford University Press, 1980). These eucharistic prayers can be read as a handy and reliable compendium of eucharistic theology. A careful study of them can provide the interested reader with a full course in eucharistic theology. They are a great treasure of theology and spirituality hallowed by centuries of usage.

A Note on Readings

Theologies of the Eucharist can be found in Joseph Powers's *Eucharistic Theology* (New York: Herder and Herder, 1967) and Tad Guzie's *Jesus and the Eucharist* (New York:

Paulist, 1974). Two works that link the Eucharist with the world of social justice are Monika K. Hellwig's *The Eucharist and the Hunger of the World* (New York: Paulist, 1976) and Tissa Balasurivya's *The Eucharist and Human Liberation* (Maryknoll, NY: Orbis, 1976). For an excellent essay on the Eucharist and further bibliography, see Raymond Molony's article "Eucharist," in *The New Dictionary of Theology*, edited by Joseph A. Komonchak et al. (Wilmington, DE: Glazier, 1987), pp. 342–55.

Behind a good deal of my thinking is the now classic work of Edward Schillebeeckx: *Christ the Sacrament of the Encounter with God* (New York: Sheed and Ward, 1963).

Bernard Cooke's *Ministry to Word and Sacraments: History and Theology* (Philadelphia: Fortress, 1976) is a comprehensive study of the Eucharist in relationship to the ministry.

There is an excellent chapter on the Eucharist, written from an Anglican perspective, in Kenneth Leech's *Experiencing God: Theology as Spirituality* (San Francisco: Harper and Row, 1985).

I was much impressed with (and indebted to) Nathan Mitchell's historical study *Cult and Controversy: The Worship of the Eucharist Outside of Mass* (New York: Pueblo, 1982). *Christian Spirituality: High Middle Ages and Reformation*, edited by Jill Raitt (New York: Crossroad, 1987), has three essays that are especially pertinent to our topic: Richard Kieckehefer's "Major Currents in Late Medieval Devotion," pp. 75–109; "Liturgy and Eucharist: East" by Robert Taft, pp. 415–26; and James McCue's "Liturgy and Eucharist: West," pp. 427–38. For earlier developments, see Pierre-Marie Gy, "Sacraments and Liturgy in Latin Christianity," in *Christian Spirituality: Origins to the Twelfth Century*, edited by Bernard McGinn et al. (New York: Crossroad, 1985), pp. 365–81. Also, Edward J. Kilmartin, *The Eucharist in the Primitive Church* (Englewood Cliffs, NJ: Prentice-Hall, 1965).

The classic work on the liturgy in Catholicism is, of course, Josef Jungmann's *The Mass of the Roman Rite*, 2 vols. (New York: Benziger, 1951).

7

MODELS

*I don't believe in saints; show me a
real saint guy.*

Frank Zappa

The Christian model of prayer is, as we have already argued, Jesus. Nonetheless the Christian tradition gives full evidence that many persons have so understood the life of prayer that their lives (and, in many cases, their prayers) have provided inspiration for others. They are, in short, models. Our very vocabulary testifies to this fact. We speak of Ignatian prayer or Sanjuanista meditation or Franciscan simplicity and so on. In all of these cases we pay implicit tribute to those who have been able to draw out of the tradition new depths of communication with God. In almost all of these cases we appreciate (and emulate) not only the methods but the lives of these religious virtuosi; they show us a way and a way to be because we recognize in them examples of the pray-er *par excellence.* Quite often these models provide us with an exemple of living as well as with a body of spiritual doctrine or a method of prayer. In this chapter we simply want to express in some detail what it means for us to look to these models of the Christian (and, often, non-Christian) spiritual life.

In an influential essay (see the reading list at the end of the chapter) Steven Katz has argued, against the conventional wisdom, that mystics are rarely suspect outsiders in a given religious tradition. In fact they contribute to, and are part of, the conservative character of religious traditions. While pressing that argument, Katz discusses mystics and contemplative masters/mistresses as paradigms for a given religious tradition. He sets out a goodly number of ways in which these virtuosi serve as models. We will start this discussion with an abridged summary of those ways. We will set them out in the order that Katz discusses them. It will be obvious from this listing that Jesus continues to stand as the preeminent model, but that those others who enjoy a place in the pantheon of the Catholic tradition can, appropriately, also find their place. According to Katz, such persons:

1. Provide a model of the attitudes and practices that others can appropriate or imitate. For Christians, this is preeminently true of Jesus and, in turn, those who follow after Jesus in imitation of him.

2. Reflect an existential representation of a given tradition. Thus, a Francis of Assisi shows, in his life, how one might live out a certain strain of the Gospel tradition. This notion goes back to our earlier observations about how the tradition enfleshes even small observations of the Gospel into a way of life.

3. Demonstrate that a doctrinal tradition can be fleshed out in life; saints turn doctrine into praxis. Again, to cite Saint Francis, one finds in his life a *theologia crucis* acted out in his life in general and in the stigmata in particular.

4. Provide "proof" that a tradition is still viable, believable, and imitable. A Thomas Merton shows in his life that a deep contemplative life is still possible in contemporary society in the West. In that sense, models are able to retrieve the past traditions of a religious community.

5. Stand as a prophetic criticism of the prevailing religious culture. In this paradigm, the model may be at sharp odds with the reigning orthodoxies, cultural and religious, of the day. Only time and the tradition domesticate the revolutionary insights of the great saints and mystics.

6. May, but do not necessarily, bring a new revelation to a religious tradition. That is most conspicuously the case in the life of Jesus who deepens the Hebrew knowledge of God through the *Abba* experience. It can also be considered true of the saints if we understand revelation with a lower case *r*

that stands for insight or affirmation of a forgotten side of the Gospel message.

7. May bring a new deepening or new approach to a received religious tradition. Thus, a Mother Teresa witnesses to the value of religious life traditionally conceived and lived. This paradigm has an obvious relationship with (4). In both cases, such saints serve "conservative" functions within the believing community.

8. May have a transtemporal modality imputed to him/her. Thus, Mary is a historical person, but the Catholic tradition also sees her as contemporaneous with the religious experiences of each generation. Mary, in the traditional devotional life of the Catholic tradition, holds a privileged place because of what she did and who she was in the economy of salvation and, also, because she serves as a transhistorical model for other ages.

9. Are models that can become founders of religious communities. This is frequent in the Catholic tradition where contemplative virtuosi channel their energies into communities that often bear their names (e.g., the Benedictine family). This function in the Catholic tradition has served as an outlet for sectarian impulses while still maintaining the essential unity of the great church.

10. Provide an authoritative picture of "reality" that can be seen as normative for the religious community. The way a Saint Vincent de Paul lived is the way we should live, for example, if we wish to show concern for the poor in our immediate community.

11. Show what the deepest meaning of being "human" really is. It is a commonplace in the Christian spiritual tradition that religious virtuosi manifest or attempt to reach the "peak" of human fulfillment, as for instance the "angelic life" (bios angelikos) of the early ascetic or the "true self" of the contemporary mystic or as one who has been transformed in Christ in a habitual manner.

12. Provide a bridge between life here and life above. We should not underestimate the symbolic role of the model as mediator, or axis mundi, for the believing community. It is from that insight that the whole structure of the saints in in-

tercessory prayer finds its origins. It also explains, as Peter Brown has made abundantly clear in his studies of early ascetics, how the religious model can act as a mediator between two planes of reality being, for example, a conduit for divine power and favor. A great deal of the interest in saints in the early church derived precisely from this mediatorial function.

13. Provide a moral paradigm for religious living and the ethical behavior demanded by such living. The martyrs, for example, show that, in the face of evil, one must (and *can*) say a resounding "No!" even at the expense of life itself. Everyone may not have the moral stamina of the martyr, but the precise function of the martyr beyond his or her own witness is to show that we lack such stamina. In that sense they also have a prophetic role in a religious community vis-à-vis those who are less inclined to wager all on religious commitments.

When we look over the rather schematic list given above, two things become quite clear. First, the religious model stands in a tradition and, secondly, the religious model extends or expands or deepens the tradition. Every great model, which is to say, every great saint, manifests a dialectical dynamic with respect to the religious tradition that can be described as radically innovative: radical in the sense that the saint is profoundly rooted in a tradition, and innovative in the sense that new insights are brought forward and/or emphasized that have either been overshadowed or neglected. To paraphrase a line from the Gospel: The saint brings forth new things and old.

That dynamic operates even in the most traditional examples one cares to cite. Mother Teresa of Calcutta has attracted the admiration of the contemporary world (as well as some detractors) even outside the church. When one looks at her life it is evident that what she does has a certain atemporal quality to it in the sense that one could imagine her doing exactly what she does today a thousand years ago. Mother Teresa stands in a long line of apostles of charity who have garlanded the church over the centuries. Her program is simply to lavish an evangelical love on those who are, naturally speaking, the least likely to be loved: the destitute poor, the discarded dying, and those wounded in body and spirit. In that sense her work and witness is very traditional. The fact that she does it today, however, and not centuries ago is a sign that such work(s) and its spiritual underpinnings are not anachronistic. The spirituality she invokes (and vigorously insists upon) still manages to attract others despite its "traditional" character. Paradoxically, her innovation is to be traditional in a time of upheaval and change. In that sense, she gives vitality to the perennial values of the church tradition.

By contrast, the long view of the Christian tradition provides us with many examples of people who were innovative in the ordinary sense of the term. When we look at the innovative character of their lives, however, what we inevitably see is rootedness in an early tradition transformed through the alchemy of their particular genius and the *Zeitgeist* that produced them. Thus, to cite a conspicuous example, Ignatius of Loyola (1491–1556) conceived of a religious movement that would depart radically from the earlier tradition of monasticism and the mendicant orders of the medieval period. Furthermore, the program of spirituality he set out in *The Spiritual Exercises* made a dramatic break with the older tradition of contemplation as its own end in favor of a mysticism that would evolve into action. Historians are unanimous in their perception of Ignatius as a powerful innovator who stands at the very fountainhead of post-Reformation renewal in the Roman Catholic church. Careful readers of church history must train themselves to see how innovative people were who now are safely enshrined in the tradition. It is a good sociological rule (formulated by a number of people) that canonization is one way to domesticate and control innovation and charisma.

Despite this deserved reputation for creative innovation, it must be equally noted that the spirituality of Ignatius did not spring from his life free of antecedents and deep traditional roots. We know both from his autobiography (dictated to a fellow Jesuit in the last decade of his life) and other sources that the books which were most influential in his life were of the most traditional sort: a life of Christ by the German Carthusian, Ludolf of Saxony; the *Golden Legend*, a medieval compilation of lives of the saints by Jacopus da Voragine; and, above all, the *Imitation of Christ* of Thomas à Kempis. Furthermore, in the early days of his converted life he adapted styles of life that are almost traditional clichés: the knight, the pilgrim, the hermit, the student. In other words, what would become *Saint* Ignatius of Loyola was undergirded by medieval piety, the late medieval *devotio moderna*, traditional paradigms of spiritual living (recall that Francis of Assisi was also a hermit for a period and used knightly imagery to describe his life), and a thirst to act for the Kingdom of God. Refined by his spiritual genius and the times in which he lived, what resulted was not a blend of the old, but something quite new, supple, and perfectly apt for the times, but not independent of the traditions that were in the culture in his lifetime.

Those who model prayer for us are, whether contemporary or historical, very much the products of their own history as well as the history that shaped them both within the Christian tradition and in their general culture. Thus, a distinction must be made between those things that are accidental in a model and those things that are central. If one wants to adopt the monastic practice of *lectio* as a part of the life of prayer, it is not equally necessary to adopt a cowl, a rubricated psalter, or the other epiphenomena with which the popular mind imagines monastic life: *habitus monachum non creat.*

By a similar logic one cannot ordinarily utilize the writings of the spiritual masters/mistresses in contemporary experience without some willingness to "translate" their experiences into a language that we understand in a cultural sense which goes beyond the verbal. Very few people today would be able to "use" the language or replicate the imaginings of the Little Flower, Thérèse of Lisieux. Her piety is expressed in a language that reflects a kind of nineteenth-century sentimentalism which is alien to the modern mind. Nonetheless, when one translates the Gospel values in Thérèse by a sympathetic and critical understanding of her life (as writers like Hans Urs von Balthasar and Joann Wolski Conn have done so successfully), we can retrieve values from the Little Way which are fresh and pertinent to Christians generally and women in particular, as Conn so persuasively argues.

How do we, in fact, make that translation? How do we reach across the ages to recover the wisdom of the desert anchorites or the medieval mystics or the post-Reformation activists? At one level the answer is fairly obvious. We take those things that have come to us from the tradition and adapt them to the needs and conditions of the present. The church has always renewed itself by a return to its sources as a process of retrieval. Thus, for example, there has been an intense effort to recapture the contemplative methods of the fourteenth-century English mystics in the practice of centering prayer, and religious families like the Carmelites and the Jesuits have reappropriated their spiritual masters/mistresses in the light of the theological, patristic, and scriptural advances of the present era.

There is the further task of remembering that which has been forgotten or thrust to the margins by either the neglect or the suppressive powers of those who presume to speak for the tradition. Nowhere has this movement to remember and recall been more persistent than in the flourishing field of feminist studies of theology and religion. In the past decade or so there has been a veritable revolution in scholarship as persons in the Catholic tradition, who had been viewed as peripheral to the shape of the tradition or relegated to the corners of piety, have now begun to receive attention so as to rescue their stories for both a more complete picture of the tradition and as a matrix for the concerns of contemporary persons. A good deal of this scholarship has been done in the area of history, but the results of this research have (and will continue to have) an enormous impact on contemporary Christian living.

One of the more conspicuous results of this scholarly retrieval is a move away from the more narrow concerns with theology strictly considered to a more holistic attempt to see how theology was worked out in the actual life experiences of people. Such studies, often done by nontheologians, enrich the tradition in the sense that they bring theology back to a richer presentation in which the lived experience of the encounter with Christ becomes paramount. Such presentations help to narrow the gap, lamentable as it, between the academic study of theology and the less-well-described field of spirituality.

In a recent pathfinding study entitled *Fire and Light: The Saints and Theology*, William H. Thompson argues passionately for the recognition that the saints offer a legitimate but neglected *locus* for theological reflection. Thompson not only argues for the legitimacy of such an enterprise but also offers a way into such an area. Borrowing from the insights of a number of contemporary theologians (especially David Tracy), he argues for a "conversation" between the saint and contemporary experience. Such a conversation, of course, does not mean simply an inquiry into what a particular saint "said" to her age but how the life and example of that life reach across the age(s) to speak to us. Such an interpretative strategy, not dissimilar to what the biblical exegete or the theologian does, is less interested in an archaeological reconstruction than in an attempt to ask what these figures, with their surplus meaning, might have to offer to those who live in different times and different days: How do they, metaphorically speaking, "speak across" the chasms of history and culture?

Such a conversation, as Thompson makes clear, involves speech on my side and on the side of the saint/model. We bring to the past example of the saints our own queries, doubts, hesitations, aspirations, and failures in order to sort out the resonances with their experiences that may provide some help with our own life of prayer. This conversation, it hardly needs saying, must be capable of separating out that which is culture-bound from the conversation. To read John of the Cross or Thérèse of Lisieux is not to find ways of becoming a Carmelite but to discover avenues of prayer.

A practical example may help to give flesh to this notion of conversation. There is a tradition in the writings of the great spiritual masters and mistresses of prayer that emphasizes the desolation inherent in prayer. Such a stage of desolation or darkness is seen as a necessary part of deepening prayer. It is the cloud that is described in mystical treatises from Gregory of Nyssa to the unknown author of the fourteenth-century *Cloud of Unknowing*. It appears in Saint John of the Cross as the "dark night" (the *noche oscura*) of the soul. The analyses of this phenomenon are common in the literature of prayer. Without specifying rigid categories on the phenomenon, we can say that this desolation carries with it an implied need to purify oneself from a disordered life as well as a need to stay firm in faith even when the consolations of faith are absent. The *noche oscura* is the condition that occurs when we pray despite the deep conviction that God is absent or silent or unresponsive to us. It is *sheer* prayer in the face of a void that seems either indifferent or nonexistent. At its most acute, as a number of people have noted, it is like the anguish of a deeply regretted atheism.

Ignacio Larranaga's recent *Sensing Your Hidden Presence* suggests that this traditional sense of desolation might be understood in the modern context as a detachment of the theoretical acceptance of the existence of God from God as encountered in prayer. It is an argument, obviously, that is consonant with this entire book. Father Larranaga's argument is that religious faith which is not anchored in prayer brings with it a species of existential atheism, which is to say, a life that, for all practical purposes, is cut loose from the anchor of existence, which is God. In that sense, desolation is anterior to prayer or, to put it in Father Larranaga's words, when we stop praying, God becomes a "nobody" precisely because in this practical atheism there is an absence of relationship. I am here and God is there, but no bridge—at least from the human perspective—links the two.

In that sense, at least, we can understand the desolation of the mystical tradition not simply as a way station on the road to contemplation but as a deeply felt obstacle when we feel (or do not feel) inclined to pray. In that sense the general culture itself (hardly conducive to prayer) can be seen as a contextual form of desolation carrying with it that anomie which makes prayer seem, not impossible, but simply absurd. The character of that boredom has been caught perfectly in John Dalrymple's *Simple Prayer:*

> You cannot say to yourself: this is God's design, all is well, because you are in the process of doubting whether God exists and whether there is such a design. Christianity appears to be a fairy tale, with any number of psychological explanations. You feel you have been deceived about God and about prayer, that any experiences you may have had in the past were self-

induced, perhaps escape mechanisms to justify not getting involved in the life of action. The whole "God" business seems to be a sham. Yet you plod on in bewilderment, hoping against hope, and believing against belief.

Such an understanding of the desolation in prayer of which the tradition speaks is quite consonant with its understanding of the matter. It is traditional to insist that the purifying purpose of such desolation is to encourage people to pray not for the consolation of prayer but through pure faith. The great lesson of the doctrine of Saint John of the Cross, derived from his experience, is that when, by every human indication, prayer seemed useless and arid, he continued to pray. Across the ages, our conversation with John tells us, by his example and in his writing, that the desolation which accompanies prayer is neither reason to despair of oneself nor of one's prayer. That lesson transcends sixteenth-century psychology or any scholastic analysis of the path of prayer. It is a constant of the prayer experience itself.

In the above example we have been speaking about doctrine, i.e., what a particular model wrote or thought. There is, however, another way of understanding a model: by focusing on the person's style of life. Many have attempted, for example, to lead a life of poverty after the manner of Saint Francis of Assisi, just as others have been impressed by the life of solitude of the monastic tradition. This is a very old form of spiritual instruction that roots itself, ultimately, in the desire of Christians to imitate the life of Christ. We should be aware of how powerful a model can be. Saint Augustine tells us (in the *Confessions*), for example, that when he was on the verge of conversion it was the example of Saint Anthony of the desert, as he learned of it from the biography of Athanasius, that convinced him of the desirability of a life of retirement and contemplation. A millennium later, Ignatius of Loyola credits part of his conversion to a reading of the lives of the saints in the medieval compilation of Jacopus de Voragine known as *The Golden Legend*.

What the great saints of our tradition tell us, to borrow a phrase from the late Karl Rahner, is that it is possible to follow God in *this* way. That same tradition of holiness should also warn us that certain styles of life and/or styles of prayer are very much culture-bound. It is not immediately clear that this age would look upon Saint Simon Stylites with anything but bemusement. A saint on a pillar would be fodder for the tabloids, not a source of edification for the faithful. The point should be emphasized, in short, that a model is not a template to reproduce "lifestyles" with exactly similar dimensions and characteristics.

Positively speaking, the great models of prayer speak to us in a variety of ways once we have entered into conversation with their lives, and once we have acquired the sophistication to detach the essence of their message from their historical surroundings. Their lives are a kind of risk that encourages us to think of alternative ways of living, other paths to follow.

In the first instance, and generally speaking, the great saints tell us boldly and without equivocation that prayer is a possibility in life. The enormous attraction of many for such near contemporaries as the late Thomas Merton and others rests precisely in their value as a countersign to those who insist that we live in an ineluctably secular age. Their lives give warrant to our own willingness to pray and assurance that the tradition of prayer is not dead or immobile. In that same way, as a kind of other side of the coin, their very presence in our midst challenges us that, if we are believers, we must also pray. At that level the great saints are emblematic of the life of prayer and sacraments in that their sign-value as pray-ers is efficacious. It is a quasi-empirical fact that people who are profoundly prayerful attract others to them if only because they seem to testify to something that others would like to believe in or have a part of.

It is because of their witness to the centrality of prayer that the church in its liturgy invokes the saints as part of the great community (i.e., the Communion of Saints) which renders honor to God. While the saints serve as eschatological signs of our own hopes for salvation we should also recognize that they are invoked in the liturgy as *companions* of prayer. It is for that reason we pray at the liturgy to have "some share in the fellowship of your apostles and martyrs"; that we beg to praise God "in union with them"; and why, finally, we are bold to ask "to share in the inheritance of all of your saints."

Seen from that perspective, the saints function as individuals who may nourish us on this pilgrimage as well as a community that prays with us. Under the rubric of the saint as sign or emblem there is room both for the patron or model (a very traditional notion in Catholic Christianity) and for the body of saints who are fellow pray-ers joined to us as part of the Mystical Body that worships God in time and space.

Secondly, models, in their very lives, teach us how to pray better and how to live the life of prayer. They not only exemplify the possibility of prayer but become the pedagogues of prayer. "Go and join a man who fears God," Abba Poemen, one of the early desert monks, advised an inquirer, "and live near him; he will teach you, too, to fear God."

Peter Brown, in his seminal studies of the function of holy people in the early church, has argued persuasively that they not only served as mediators and charismatic leaders for the early Christian communities but also had the further role of being living icons of Christ. People looked to them to see how a living *representatio Christi* ought to look and act. It was from their example that people could see Gospel values fleshed out in the concrete exigencies of everyday life. Nor does Brown think that such a function is bound only to history. In a recent essay (see the reading list at the end of this chapter) reflecting on his work on these people Brown writes of their continuing pertinence:

> Until comparatively recently it has been habitual to dismiss Byzantine hagiography as an interesting rubbish-tip to be picked over by historians of social conditions and popular beliefs. I would strongly recommend, however, that an hour spent in the company of Pachomius, an Abba Sisoes, or a Saint Martin can tell us, more than a whole course in dogmatics, how to begin to answer a challenge posed by Dietrich Bonhoeffer almost a half a century ago, a challenge that is, half a century later, more pressing: "It is becoming clear every day that the most urgent problem besetting our church is this: how can we live the Christian life in the modern world?"

What Peter Brown observes of late antique Christianity is, by analogy, equally true of the later tradition of the church. If we assume as axiomatic the notion that the tradition of the saints is, in essence, a tradition which tries to flesh out in life the imitation of Christ, we can see that tradition as analogous to the church's long meditation on the scriptures. Every age brings to that tradition its own needs and its own insights, but breaks within the tradition occur rarely if at all. The saintly tradition in a given period may emphasize a particular facet of the following of Christ. No age can lay claim to the total picture. In that sense, we all reach up to, but never completely grasp, the total Christ.

The manner in which we "see" Christ greatly determines the character of our prayer. The intensely human Christ of the synoptic tradition is not the cosmic Christ of the Pauline tradition. Both traditions have had their appeal and both are rooted in the saintly witness of our common heritage. Those great contemporary figures who wish to dialogue with the religious traditions of the East have tended, almost connaturally, to turn to the *Pantocrator* through whom all is created and through which the universe is sustained. By contrast, the tradition of liberation theology coming from Latin America has set forth the radical Christ of the Gospels who identifies with the poor and the marginal in a bond of love which is tied to *Abba*. Obviously, these approaches to Christ produce quite different spiritualities, but both have their prior witnesses in the long tradition of the church.

The choice of a spirituality is not an exclusionary one. The radical devotion to the Christ of the synoptics needs the check of a high Christology to avoid turning devotion into mere admiration, just as cosmic Christologies needs always keep in mind the Word who was made flesh to keep from moving into abstractions and angelism. As usual, G. K. Chesterton was on target when he remarked that a Saint Francis of Assisi was the very opposite of a philanthropist, since the latter loves anthropoids but a Francis of Assisi loved this particular person existing in the concreteness of a leper or a beggar. The saint, in short, is a kind of concrete example who helps us to see how a specific form of Christian living is possible and how it can be lived out in actual life.

In the historic tradition of Catholicism Mary, the mother of the Lord, holds a privileged place as model and examplar. Mariology is a complex tradition, fraught with exaggerations and flights of the imagination, but as a tradition it has a place in the theological development of the Christian community. Mary serves as a model in life and as a source of "doctrine," especially the doctrine of prayer.

As a model Mary has been set before the Christian people in a series of set pieces, each with its significance in the life of prayer. For a millennium the art of both East and West depicted the Virgin as seated holding the child, with both of them depicted in a frontal position. This scene, heavily indebted to the theological affirmation that Mary was *Theotokos* (the "God bearer") carried with it a whole host of ancillary meanings that bore directly on the spiritual life. Mary becomes a symbol of the church who brings forth Christ, as Mary once did in the economy of history; Mary as the symbol of the Christian who, through grace, causes Christ to be born anew in the world; Mary as the Christ bearer who becomes a symbol of the missionary message of the church, etc.

The fundamental *topos* of the *Theotokos* in art did not exhaust the symbolic value of Mary as exemplar in the spiritual life. Christian art and piety took moments from her life in the Gospels to illustrate correlations for the Christian in his or her development in the life of prayer. The innumerable Annunciations of our artistic patrimony not only recalled a moment in the Gospels but were insistent reminders of the need for human consent—for a *fiat* on the part of everyone who is moved by the grace of God. The medieval theme of the Virgin at the foot of the cross not only was a paradigm for lovers of the passion but had also symbolized, from the days of early monasticism, the need for *penthos,* or grief, for sin—such *penthos* being the necessary condition of the contemplative soul. Mary as the new Eve (a theme announced in Christian theology as early as the second century) was a summing up of the spiritual life: the overcoming of sin in order to be identified with the redemptive graces of Christ. Mary, finally, took on an eschatological value as Christian piety identified her with the Woman of the Book of Revelations. She was the sure sign of our own hope for final union with Christ. As early as the second century Mary was seen as the new Eve who brought forth not sin but grace into the world. It would be possible to write a history of Marian devotion just by looking carefully at the evolution of the visual arts about her.

The Christian tradition, as many have noted, turned to the Virgin and "read" into her life the preeminent virtues of the reigning culture. For the early centuries Mary could serve as the perfect contemplative, while in the high medieval period she was the paradigm of the Lady who was to be greeted with courtesy and, in return, she would be the giver of graces. In the Renaissance, and largely under Franciscan influences, Mary was seen as the quintessential mother who, in her Raphaelite representations, was the ideal of maternity itself.

In our own day the place of Mary (and, especially, her role as symbol) has been much discussed. While feminist scholars have appreciated the role of Mary as a feminine dimension of piety, there has been an equal worry that the paradoxical celebration of virginity-motherhood subverts the full sexuality of women. There has been an intense interest in the place of Mary in the piety of the peasant cultures of Latin America, where her role is a sign of passivity but—and this needs emphasis—where she is also seen as a protector of the poor whose identification with the *Anawim* (the poor people of Israel) functions as a subversion of the pretensions of the powerful and the mighty. Liberation theologians, thus, look longingly at the words of her own prayer not only as an exaltation of her place in the economy of salvation but also of the power that her position brings. Mary's *Magnificat* promises that from "henceforth all generations shall call me blessed," but it ends with a promise of power:

> He has put down the mighty from their thrones
> and exalted those of low decree.
> He has filled the hungry with good things,
> and the rich he has sent empty away.
> He has helped his servant Israel,
> in remembrance of his mercy.
> As he spoke to our fathers,
> to Abraham and to his posterity forever.
> (Luke 1:51–55)

To be faithful to the role of Mary as model and exemplar, it might be well to begin with her place in the ancient believing community and, from that starting point, read back into the Gospel accounts to see what they say about her. After the ascension of the Lord, Luke tells us, the small body of believers went back to Jerusalem. He enumerates the apostles and then adds: "All these with one accord devoted themselves to prayer, together with the women, and Mary, the mother of Jesus, and with his brothers" (Acts 1:14).

The merit of starting at this point in Mary's life is that it places her within the context of those who are Christ believers. Thus, the intention of the Second Vatican Council, which placed its reflections on Mary in the document on the church, is preserved. When we think of Mary in that community, the other things the Gospels say about her point to her characteristic of being, as one theologian has written, the perfect disciple. It then becomes possible to assimilate to the life of devotion her *fiat* at the Annunciation, her intercessory power at the wedding feast of Cana, and her position at the foot of the cross. From that perspective the spiritual lessons of her life take on new resonance and power.

Models, then, illustrate for us how we can become more like Christ, and they can serve as spiritual directors in our cultivation of the life of prayer. These models may be as distant as the canon of the saints in the liturgical tradition and as close as the person(s) who inspire us or direct us in the life of prayer. Just as the disciples went to Jesus with the petition "Lord, teach us to pray," so we also go to those formed in prayer with the same request. Models both teach us, correct us by the quality of their lives, and inspire us along the way of spiritual growth.

What makes the model different from either the cultural hero or a celebrity whom we would like to emulate is that with the great models we share a sense of communion and in their lives we see a pledge of our own salvation in Christ.

First, we share communion with them. At the level of worship this is an obvious fact. Every time we participate in the liturgy our prayer is formally joined with Mary, the apostles and martyrs, the saints and all the faithful (i.e., faith-filled) who have departed this life. This point needs emphasis since too often in popular imagination the saints have been detached from this common bond of prayer and faith to be made into folk symbols (e.g., Saint Patrick) or demigods with limited powers (Saint Jude) or figures of extravagance and/or myth. The saints, first and foremost, are those who are alive in Christ and with whom we share a commonality of faith. Their faith is perfected in charity; ours is still *in via*.

The saints, secondly, point us to a goal not yet reached and in that they serve as eschatological signs. Our saintly models, in short, point us to the "not yet" of our lives. They do this in two ways. At the more immediate level, their lives and teachings show us that we can still deepen our prayer, refine our religious sensibility, turn our prayer into action, and so on. In short, they point out the limitless potentialities of the spiritual life and the ways in which those potentialities can be realized. Beyond that, our conviction that they are now "with the Lord" is a pledge of our own hope that such will be the outcome of our life. The saints, in short, aid us on the way.

There is a final point. Many people find it hard to enter into the tradition of the saints because that tradition has been refracted through art and legend in such a fashion as to have an unreal air about it. It is for that reason, I suspect, that many contemporary Catholics look to uncanonized persons for inspiration. The late Dorothy Day, for instance, was a luminously holy person, but her life included an abortion, a common-law marriage, a period of left-wing politics, and deep involvement in feminist concerns (her first arrest, before her conversion, was for suffragette activities). People see in her life the traumas and challenges of twentieth-century life as a background to her passionate holiness cast in an authentically Franciscan mode.

One need not even invoke a "celebrity" model like Dorothy Day. It has been one of my strongest convictions that one could go to any corner of the church's life and find people who are transcendently holy and deep pray-ers. Every parish priest knows of these hidden saints who live urban or rural or suburban lives with a vivid sense of the presence of God.

When we search our own histories and our own memories we can usually locate a person, sometimes a family member, sometimes a friend or teacher or neighbor, whose lives give witness to the authenticity of prayer and the reality of Christ's love in the world. Someone would do the church a great service by collecting a representative sample of the life stories of these hidden saints to show the truth of the church's claim that one of its distinguishing marks is holiness.

It is to those people that we turn in the life of Christian living. They may serve as models from afar or they may function as what the early Celtic Christians called, beautifully, a "soul-friend" who shares with us the spiritual journey. To those people we turn as we live out the life of prayer. On the value of that task we can turn again to a saying of Abba Poemen, one of the early desert fathers, since in his brevity he puts the matter squarely and without adornment:

> A brother asked Abba Poemen, "Some brothers live with me; do you want me to be in charge of them?" The old man said to him, "No, just work first and foremost, and if they want to live like you they will see it themselves." The brother said to him, "But it is they themselves, Father, who want me to be in charge of them." The old man said to him, "No, be their example, not their legislator."

A Prayer

> O Almighty God, who has knit together thine elect in one communion and fellowship, in the Mystical Body of thy Son Christ Our Lord; grant us the grace so to follow thy blessed saints in all virtuous living that we may come to those unspeakable joys, which thou has prepared for them that unfeignedly love thee; through Jesus Christ Our Lord. Amen.

This prayer, taken from the Anglican *Book of Common Prayer* (1662), sums up succinctly what I have tried to say in this chapter. The saints are seen not as discrete virtuosi existing in a separate company but as dwelling in the communion and *koinonia* (fellowship) with all who are in Christ Jesus. Furthermore, they are recalled for two reasons. First, they serve as models for the Christian life and, secondly, through an imitation of their virtues we hope for the blessedness that they now enjoy.

Embedded in that short prayer, then, are both individual and corporate elements: individual, in the sense that the saints can serve as models for us on our spiritual path, and corporate in that we are all bound ("knit together") as a confessing community.

That brief collect reflects a deep strain in all Catholic liturgies. Whether it be the canon of the Roman liturgy or the eucharistic commemorations of the Liturgy of St. John Chrysostom (Byzantine), there is a constant reminder that all who are "in the Lord" constitute the meaning of the saints at the deepest level and, as a consequence, they are signs of hope and examples for life for all of us who are still on pilgrimage.

A Note on Readings

An exhaustive essay on the saints may be found in *Saints and Their Cults*, edited by Stephen Wilson (New York: Cambridge University Press, 1983). My own longer reflections on the saints as models may be found in *The Meaning of Saints* (San Francisco: Harper and Row, 1980). For the ways in which mystics can serve as models and/or paradigms, see Steven T. Katz, "The 'Conservative' Character of Mystical Experience," in *Mysticism and Religious Traditions*, edited by Steven T. Katz (New York: Oxford University Press, 1983), pp. 3–61. My book *The Catholic Heritage* (New York: Crossroad, 1983) has attempted to survey Catholic history from the perspective of paradigms and/or ideal types.

William M. Thompson's *Fire and Light: The Saints and Theology* (Mahwah, NJ: Paulist, 1987) is a sustained argument for making the saints into a *locus theologicus*. See also Karl Rahner, "The Church of the Saints," in *Theological Investigations* 3 (Baltimore: Helicon, 1967), pp. 91–105, for a consideration of the saint as a model for new ways of being religious. Peter Brown's essay "The Saint as Exemplar in Late Antiquity," in *Saints and Virtues*, edited by John Stratton Hawley (Berkeley: University of California, 1987), pp. 3–14, reflects on his earlier work and advances his notion of the saint as an imitator of Christ. In that same collection, there is an excellent essay summing up the interdisciplinary work of the scholars collected in the volume: John A. Coleman's "Conclusion: After Sainthood?" pp. 205–26. *Liturgy* devoted an entire issue in 1985 (vol. 5, no. 2) to the saints from the liturgical perspective. There are nineteen essays in the issue. For a more phenomenological study of the saints, see *Sainthood: Its Manifestation in World Religions*, edited by Richard Kieckhefer and George D. Bond (Berkeley, CA: University of California Press, 1988).

The citations from the early desert ascetics are taken from *The Sayings of the Desert Fathers: The Alphabetical Collection*, edited by Benedicta Ward (Kalamazoo, MI: Cistercian Publications, 1975).

The two books on prayer referred to in this chapter are: John Dalrymple, *Simple Prayer* (Wilmington: Glazier, 1984) and Ignacio Larranaga, *Sensing Your Hidden Presence: Toward Intimacy With God* (Garden City, NY: Doubleday, 1987).

The notion of the "soul-friend" has received a full treatment in Kenneth Leech, *Soul Friend: The Practice of Christian Spirituality* (San Francisco: Harper and Row, 1980).

The literature on Mary is immense. I have been much aided by both the text and bibliography of Patrick J. Bearsley's "Mary the Perfect Disciple," *Theological Studies* 41 (September 1980), pp. 461–504. Hilda Graef's older historical survey has recently been reissued: *Mary: A History of Doctrine and Devotion* (Westminster, MD: Christian Classics, 1987). I have expressed myself on this topic in *Mother of God* (San Francisco: Harper and Row, 1981). For a more recent, but limited, historical survey, see Elizabeth A. Johnson, "Marian Devotion in the Western Church," in *Christian Spirituality: High Middle Ages and Reformation*, edited by Jill Raitt (New York: Crossroad, 1987), pp. 392–415. There is a wealth of material in Michael O'Carroll's *Theotokos: A Theological Encyclopedia of the Blessed Virgin Mary* (Wilmington: Glazier, 1983).

8

POLITICS

*What is purity? It is a heart which
has compassion on every natural thing in creation.*

Saint Isaac of Nineveh

At the outset let it be noted that this chapter will not
deal with politics if, by that term, one understands the spectrum that runs from statecraft as a high abstraction to the
practice of politics at the local level. Nor by politics will I
assay the recent attempts to construct a "political theology"
or any of the varieties of liberation theology which are, I take
it, subspecies of political theology. This disclaimer is made at
the outset not because I am apolitical, but because the topic
is so complex and discussions of it so heated and *parti pris*
that I am not sure anything I would add to it would be more
than an excursus following the phrase "In my opinion ... "
Furthermore, I do not want here to enter into those somewhat
overheated debates, now so common in this country, as to
whether the church should identify its fortunes with various
wings of political thinking. Those debates are bracing but not
germane to what this chapter hopes to achieve. I am more
interested in general principles and less interested in particular strategies.

So that this chapter does not seem to have a misplaced title
let me positively state that by politics I mean, simply, the
term in its etymological sense: that which concerns the *polis*
as opposed to the individual. What I would like to meditate
upon is the connecting link between prayer—my prayer—in

relation to the larger community of which I am a part. Furthermore, I will take the term *community* to mean social bonds in the most generous sense of the term. In that sense, community expands, as it were, in concentric circles from the intimate bonds of family and neighborhood—the domestic church—to the great church and the world. It is, in that somewhat generous sense, that I understand the term *politics*.

When the poet observed (in a sermon, let it be remembered!) that no person is an "island unto himself" he was stating a truth that is fundamental to the point of being a truism. By nature, humans are social beings and their sociability runs out in concentric circles from the more intimate to the more global. James Joyce caught that very nicely when, in *A Portrait of the Artist as a Young Man* he has his hero, Stephen Dedalus, coming to his own personal sense of individuality at an early age. In one of his grammar-school books the novel's protagonist writes in the flyleaf:

Stephen Dedalus
Class of Elements
Clongowes Wood College
Sallins
County Kildare
Ireland
Europe
The World
The Universe

We can all do variations on this theme. What Joyce (or his contemporaries) did not have to add into his computation was the element of dependence on the world apart from Europe. Notice that from Europe Stephen thought immediately of the world. The rest of the globe was not considered; it was, at worst, *terra incognita* or, if recognized at all, dusky lands under colonial dominion.

Today we, if we are reflective, cannot be so parochial. A personal survey of one's circumstances makes the point effortlessly. I sit at my word processor (assembled here in the USA with chips from Japan) in a pair of Levis sewn in Mexico while wearing British brand sneakers (Reeboks) which, a discrete tag tells me, were manufactured in South Korea. For lunch, I will eat salad from vegetables grown in the southern part of Florida which were harvested by a vast army of laborers who are Hispanic or contracted for the work from one of the Caribbean islands. The ordinary circumstances of my not uncomfortable life, in short, depend on vast numbers of people who are alien to me in culture, language, and economic status. I am bound to them in my needs and they, in turn, are bound to me by the absolute imperative of human survival. We do not always advert to those dependencies, but that does not mean that they are not there. The bald fact is that they are.

The enormous web of economic dependence that surrounds all of us points to a fact: We are all part of a global economy and, despite the tough restraints of nationalism, partially enwebbed in a world culture. This fact intrudes on our life in only peripheral ways until the machinery develops a glitch: the oil on which we depend does not arrive at our shores, or other countries decide not to finance our debt. Then, our comfortable lives can become ominously threatened. It takes crisis—usually economic crisis—to underscore how enwebbed we are in the larger world. There is no way to avoid this fact unless one belongs to that diminishing group of purely tribal people who inhabit remote (but ever-less remote!) regions of the world.

And what does all this have to do with prayer? I would not be so banal as to suggest that we ought to pray for the workers who sew our shoes or stoop to harvest our crops, although if we could pray with them (instead of simply for them) it would be an extension of our catholicity. If, however, we accept that to pray is to do something truly human or, to phrase it better, to be truly human, prayer should be part of the spectrum of who we are. We cannot ignore the fact that we are political beings in the sense we have described: We belong to the *polis*, and that *polis* is very large and becoming larger with each passing decade. This expansion comes despite the fact that we tend to think of ourselves in only a local or parochial sense.

The Catholic tradition has always recognized that fact. From the beginnings our liturgy has prayed for both the church and for the civil *polis;* we pray for everyone from the pope to all legitimate rulers. The social character of liturgical prayer is written into our earliest liturgies. The *Didache* sees in the broken bread of the Eucharist a symbol of the church which is to "be brought together from the ends of the earth into your Kingdom." Justin, a second-century apologist, writes in his *First Apology* that the worshiping assembly gathers "to make common prayers earnestly for ourselves and for him who has been enlightened [i.e., the baptized], for all others everywhere, that, having learned the truth, we may be deemed worthy to be found good citizens and guardians of the commandments." In the same *Apology* Justin notes that the offerings of the wealthy are distributed by the leader of the community to widows, orphans, the sick, those in prison, foreigners "sojourning among us" and "in a word, he takes care of all those who are in need." We have already noted, in an earlier chapter, that the custom of taking home the Eucharist was, in effect, a practice that was meant to extend the Eucharist out from the confines of the church itself to embrace a larger community. There is, in short, a very close connection between catholicity and politics as I have described it above.

The political character of prayer, to be brief, finds its roots in the very notion of catholicity, which means both universality in fact but, more importantly, in aspiration and outlook. We proclaim ourselves Catholic, but the fullness of that catholicity is always ahead of us. We have warrant for that fact in that a number of theologians have pointed to the profound shifts taking place in our very concept of how the church stands in history. Karl Rahner is famous for his assertion that the Second Vatican Council marked the first step away from a European church and toward a world church. Walbert Buhlmann has enlarged that idea in his influential *The Coming of the World Church* (1977) and, more recently, in *The Church of the Future* (1986). We see one small indication of that shift in North American demographics since as, it is clear, the American church has received its greatest growth not from the old centers of Europe but from the new Hispanic centers to the South of us.

One of the most important themes in current theology is the interrelationship between the local worshiping community and the great church as a whole. The importance of this theme does not reside solely in questions of jurisprudence (e.g., how can the American church be American while, at the same time, Roman in matters of discipline?) but in terms of mutual responsibility: How does the American church relate to the Ugandan church and how do they both relate to the universal witness of Christ?

When we pray as Catholics, then, we pray for the entire church of the world and, as the Second Vatican Council insisted, for the world at large. The many attempts to dialogue with the religious traditions of the world have found their most fruitful advances when they have started from the premise of prayer. That is why scholars like William Johnston and others have insisted that it is from the basis of contemplation and prayer that Christians will be able to learn from, and be in conversation with, the ancient religious traditions of the East. The teachings of the Second Vatican Council on both ecumenism and on non-Christian religions have enlarged the prayer-arena into a global challenge for the church.

We should also note that most of us tend to look from the local church toward larger realities. We might be more sympathetic to the burdens of the papacy, to cite an obvious example, if we remember that Peter's successor must look out over the entire church, with its not always homogeneous needs, in order to make himself a universal pastor. In our case, as well as that of the pontiff's, there is a kind of spiritual geography to be considered.

The issues so briefly touched on in the above paragraphs seem so large—almost cosmic—that one could legitimately ask how the hypothetical person in the pews could come to grips with them in any way beyond giving lip service and passive acceptance to their legitimacy. Most of us are home/parish/city bound to an extent that national politics engage us only sporadically, and world politics not at all. This limitation comes, not from indifference or callousness, but from a need to get through the challenges of life as they appear to us in the concrete circumstances of our life. What most believers lack, one suspects, is not good will but the imperatives of perspective: We just do not feel compelled to think much beyond our "natural" boundaries.

There are two things at work behind the assumptions of this chapter. The first is that, by its very constitution, prayer is political, and the second is that all of us need to expand the sense in which we understand the *polis*. What seems equally clear is that connecting prayer to a stronger sense of community will not come from those who merely sermonize about it. We must eschew the "eat your dinner; think of the starving children of China" approach to a more considered way of bringing our prayer and our consciousness of community into some kind of synchronization. We must make, in short, our prayer radically *catholic*. At the deepest, most etymological sense of the term, Catholic prayer is political prayer. The term "catholic" by its own inner logic demands that we think of the *polis* broadly understood, while resisting the concept of "political" understood in the narrow sense in which we ordinarily use the term.

How, in fact, do we accomplish that?

We must begin with those familiar injunctions in the Gospels that demand a harmony between what we say and who we are and what we do. We should not pray while devouring the substance of widows, just as we should not pray for the adulation of the crowd. Matthew, chapters five through seven, spells out those disharmonies and their remedies in painfully helpful detail. It may well be that relatively few of us combine ostentatious piety with rent-gouging, but the larger examples of hypocrisy given in the Gospels are meant to teach a more refined truth: Prayer must strive to be uttered in clarity both of language and of purpose. Prayer must be constantly examined in light of the true motives of the self. Only then does it become genuine prayer. We must strive, in short, to make Catholic prayer, catholic, which is to say, universal.

For prayer to be Catholic prayer the "true motives of the self" cannot be understood in a purely individualistic way. We pray, in fact, as part of a community, which is a less-charged way of saying that all prayer is political prayer. Our foundation point, then, is to come to an awareness of that dimension of prayer. At times, the point can be made with the most rudimentary form of reflection on context. It is one thing, for example, to pray that we receive "our daily bread" while anticipating Christmas dinner, but it is quite another thing to make that same request if we are part of a famine-relief team. Context lends urgency to the phrases of piety. It is of the essence of prayer that it be recited somewhere, by someone, with a certain series of words. Prayer does not exist in a platonic nether world freed from the pressure points of historical or cultural reality. If we are to be pray-ers, we must, to be truly catholic, be political pray-ers.

Most of us, however, pray in the most ordinary of circumstances: at Mass, before retiring, before meals, and so on. Hence, we need begin at the beginning. One starting point might be to begin to cultivate a greater sense of the catholic nature of the liturgy. When we gather to celebrate the Eucharist it might be well to recall that we are doing that at roughly the same time as a large part of the world. This fact might press on our consciousness that the gathering of those who witness Christ takes place under the most diverse of conditions. We are part of a community that meets in the baroque splendors of the Vatican as well as in the most humble chapels in the Third and Fourth Worlds. The cultural circumstances are different; the act remains the same.

Once we have turned our attention to the catholic nature of worship, the words of the liturgy begin to take on a new significance and a new sharpness which can justifiably be called prophetic. When the Gospel speaks of "doing it to the least of the brethren" there is a sharpness to that proclamation once we visualize the fact that a lot of us live in a splendor which most of the world cannot imagine, much less hope for (or pray for!).

The danger in such a raising of consciousness is the temptation to abstraction. We can commiserate comfortably enough with those who are poor if the poor are some distance from us. The poor become an abstract noun which means, roughly, "not us." Is that not precisely what the scriptures have in mind when they remind us that "If any one says, 'I love God' and hates his brother, he is a liar; for he who does not love his brother whom he has seen, cannot love God whom he has not seen" (1 John 4:20).

Prayer, then, must take on specificity. At times we need to be jerked away from the complacencies of our piety. This came home to me in a compelling way while reading about the great child educator Janusz Korczak, who was the director of a Jewish orphanage in the Warsaw ghetto. In 1942 he led his children and staff through the corpse-strewn streets of the ghetto to a central loading point for deportation to the gas chambers of Treblinka. His surviving diary had this penultimate entry, which was a paraphrase of a prayer we all know:

> Our Father who art in heaven . . .
> This prayer was carved out of hunger and misery.
> Our daily bread.
> Bread.

It is a great grace to see familiar words ripped from their usual context in order to have them come back and sting us with a new freshness and depth. That becomes all the more true when someone, like a Janusz Korczak, takes those words which we have routinized and turns them upon us in the fullness of their meaning. At that level there is a great communication which shows us how paltry our understanding is when it stands only within our own perspective and framed within our finite experiences.

The great challenge is so to pray that the needs and joys of those who make up the great *polis* of human relations is a vivid reality for us. One begins to do that when he or she learns a truth stressed by the ecological movement: *Act locally but think globally.* This aphorism is a variant reflection on the well-known Catholic principle of subsidiarity.

Environmental activists adopted that motto precisely because they know that everything in the world has an interdependent link. As soon as someone worries about the purity of his or her drinking water she is forced, inevitably, to ask larger questions about the control of toxic elements in the local landfill and/or their use in a local industry, which again demands that one learn about environmental legislation or the lack thereof, and so on. By analogy, such links are common in the community of faith.

This book was begun in a medium-sized city that is a very pleasant place in which to live. The biggest employer is the state itself because this is a capitol city (hence lots of bureaucrats) with two universities and a community college which among them enroll nearly thirty-five thousand students. Those institutions require lots of well-educated professionals. Yet there are homeless people here. There is a bad cocaine problem. There are a number of dislocated and very disadvantaged people. Peter Maurin, the founder of the Catholic Workers, once said that Christians should just step outside their door and begin to do good. There are plenty of opportunities to do that in this rather nice town of mine.

When one starts to do precisely that, at however modest a level, the local act of doing good soon takes on larger dimensions. Once a week someone volunteers a few hours to help at the Saint Vincent de Paul hot-meal program for the poor. One needs to go there only a few times to begin asking questions, first to oneself, and then, in time, to others. Why are those mentally ill people left to fend for themselves on the streets? Why do we have so many people ravaged by drug and alcohol on the streets? Where do these elderly people go after the evening meal? Why are so many young families, children in tow, on the road in battered cars looking for a place to settle down with work and a roof? Questions lead to other questions; more importantly, local questions become larger questions. It again becomes an issue of concentric circles.

When these questions are asked in the context of one's life of prayer and worship they transform the character of that prayer and worship. The same thing is true of those issues that seem, at first glance, to be more "churchy" questions. When we see, for example, the not insignificant number of single mothers in a Sunday congregation (to say nothing of those who are not there!) we instinctively begin to ask not the obvious question of how the church ministers to these women but the larger question that adheres naturally to their situation: What is the place of women in the church? Does the need to raise a family include within it the right to a second marriage? If not, why not? How does the church minister, or fail to minister, to that domestic church which is the family?

To ask these questions in the context of prayer (we could, obviously, multiply the questions and the issues) is to raise very deep questions about the very nature of the Christian community itself. It has long been recognized—in a way, it is obvious—that to inquire into the social or political nature of prayer is to inquire into the character of ecclesiology. Questions of prayer—to use our example—are like questions of ecology; by nature, they reveal interdependencies.

Do we wish to think of the church as a community called out from the world so that it might stand as a countersign to the world? Is this church to be thought of as a sign-mystery of the grace of Christ which, by its very existence, makes a prophetic judgment on the world while, simultaneously, calling that world back to repentance and grace? Such a view of the church can be sustained as one that has an honorable place in the Catholic tradition. It is an understanding of the church that Avery Dulles has called "Neo-Augustinian" because of its emphasis on the dialectic of sin and grace. This view of the church carries with it a demand for a return to evangelical perfection and a critique of the modern world. Such a view of the church would carry with it a sharp sense of the profound mystery of God as well as a sharp sense of what is not church. This view of the church also tends to think of the world as something that needs to come to the church and not vice versa.

A second view of the church would emphasize community but allow for a good deal of diversity within that community, so that the values of human freedom, compassion, and openness would be affirmed and cultivated. This view would emphasize the latent values of Christian humanism embedded in the spirit of Vatican II with a plea that those values be brought to the fore in such a way that the church would mature and participate in the drama of human history. This view of the church would emphasize the church as servant rather than the church as countersign. The line between church and world in this understanding is less graphically drawn.

These divergent views of the church may not exist in any pure form, but they are, at the very least, tendencies that have an actual impact on both the competing ecclesiologies of the day and, more to the point, on our conceptions of the spiritual life and its shape. The former ecclesiology would bear down heavily on the need for formal worship, deep participation in the liturgical mysteries, and a deep sympathy with contemplative prayer. The more communion-oriented ecclesiology would not reject those emphases but would put great stress on the social consequences of liturgy, the need for contemplatives in action, and the social mission of the church as a witness to, and part of, the larger human community.

Both ecclesiologies carry with them the seeds of deformation and exaggeration. The Neo-Augustinian understanding of the church runs the risk of becoming sectarian, elitist, and self-absorbed. By contrast, the other model can turn sentimental, trendy, and absorbed into the cultural values of the moment. The traditional method of Catholicism for avoiding these extremes was to allow room for both impulses to exist. After all, traditional monasticism has a long history of witness to the mysterious reality of God, while the activist strain of the church has found outlets in everything from missionary activity or works of charity to movements interested in the pursuit of social justice. At times—the late Thomas Merton comes immediately to mind—there is a fusion of these two impulses.

One of the major preoccupations of the church in the last generation has been to find the proper balance between the essential mission of the church in relationship to the world. The inheritance of a tendency to divide rigidly the world of nature and supernature has given way to a far more incarnational orientation, which attempts to do justice to the claims of the Gospel as moving beyond history and that same Gospel as being essentially inserted into the world of history in general and our world in particular.

This more incarnationally holistic understanding of the church and its mission has been abundantly spelled out by Francis Schüssler Fiorenza in his recent *Foundational Theology* (1984). Fiorenza notes that the late Pope Paul VI's *Evange-*

lization in the Modern World (Evangelii Nuntiandi, 1974)
both insisted on and carefully distinguished the task of evangelization and the need for human liberation not by making
the latter a simple precondition of the former but by seeing
them as complementary. In Fiorenza's words: "The gospel is
incomplete without liberation just as liberation is incomplete
without the gospel."

To that analysis Pope John Paul II has added his own emphasis on personalism and the deep christological foundations
that underpin it. Again, as Fiorenza notes, one of the persistent themes of John Paul's papacy is what charity and mercy
can add to the demands of justice rather than what justice
contributes to charity and mercy. John Paul's insistent demand for conversion of heart is the dynamic that energizes
such sentiments.

The recent thrust of papal teaching, whatever the difference
of nuance or emphasis, reflects the general orientation of
Catholic thinking about the need for the church to be inserted
in the process of human development. On this development,
despite different formulations of it, there is virtual unanimity
in the church. The practical side of that consensus has made
itself evident in the role of the church in the struggle for civil
rights and social justice in countries that are both traditionally Catholic (e.g., the Philippines, Poland) and where the
Catholic presence is part of the minority (e.g., South Korea).

The post-conciliar insistence on the role of the church in
the world carries with it a concomitant obligation not to forget that this role should be rooted essentially in the imperatives of the Gospel; the church is not simply and exclusively
an agency of social change. Its role arises from the precise
moments where human structures require the insights of the
Gospel. The church cannot simply tend its own otherworldly
garden in the midst of social sin and rank injustice.

In the concrete application of the Gospel imperatives to the
actual needs of the *polis* one must carefully distinguish the
demands of the Gospel from the strategies most useful for the
proclamation of those demands. At times the "demands" are
evident. Recent attempts by a government to starve some of
its provinces into political submission by withholding food-

stuffs in a time of drought demand a "No" both out of human justice and as an imperative of the Gospel. Realpolitik and/or political strategies do not apply in such a case. The irreducible fact is that you do not starve innocent people for political advantage. Strategies of how to stop such crimes may differ but the crime itself must be resisted.

Alertness to the world and a Gospel response to it impinge on how we pray and worship. To say otherwise would be to drive a wedge between worship and praxis, a wedge that weakens both. That means, in the concrete, a continuing need to think through our theology of prayer in the light of this incarnational thrust of contemporary Catholicism. A "continuing need" means that rigorous self-reflection (done both individually and collectively) by which we attempt to overcome any chasm between what we say and how we live.

We are now more than a generation away from the conclusion of the Second Vatican Council. More than ever we have come to realize that the council was a transition point in the consciousness of Catholicism. Karl Rahner, in an influential essay, has argued that the transition has been, in a nutshell, from a church that was Occidental and Eurocentric to a church, yet fully to emerge, which is a world church. Other scholars have pointed out that we have yet to absorb fully the radical nature of this "decentering" experience. If these commentators are correct it means, inevitably, that our language, ideas behind that language, and the frame within which the language is used are in a state of flux. Who would have thought, even a generation ago, that the question of whether women can say, with integrity, "Our Father" would have been raised? We might have suspected such a question from a militant feminist at the edges of Christianity, but who would have thought that it could be raised by an Irish Catholic who was both a nun and a scripture scholar to boot? (See Sister Celine Mangan's 1984 book *Can We Still Call God "Father"*?) The fact that Sister Mangan raises the issue means that there is an issue to be resolved—an issue which concerns language and the weight that language bears and the context within which language is heard.

Even more far reaching than the problems of the church *ad intra* are the implications of the conciliar desire to expand the notion of the church in relationship to human culture. *Gaudium et Spes* calls for a more "universal form of human culture that promotes and expresses the unity of the human race" (art. 54) and a new "humanism in which man is especially defined by his responsibility for his brothers and for history" (art. 55). What can be imagined from a meditation on those assertions has staggering implications for theology in general and spirituality in particular. Do they not demand a human ecumenism that goes beyond even what the council proposed in its official documents on that topic?

There are impulses and experiments in many parts of the church today to try to think of the Christian witness in terms of this larger cultural imperative. The various liberation theologies—Asian, African, Latin American, etc.—are not only protest theologies but theologies that start from differing places and quite diverse beginnings. Furthermore, it is patent that such theologies turn, almost immediately and reflexively, to questions of prayer and worship: How do we build on the deep prayer and worship traditions of indigenous peoples in the non-Western world? How do we "translate" the liturgy into appropriate thought forms? How do we understand the relationship of answering the needs of depressed societies and the life of prayer? When does prayer become, not worship, but ideology? How does prayer disentangle itself from preoccupations with the self and the requirements of the self?

To those profound issues raised by theologies written in the non-Eurocentric world there are others that are occasioned by our far more positive view of the non-Christian religions of the world. Catholics have been in dialogue with this world for well over a century. We have seen men and women who went to non-Christian worlds not to convert aggressively (although conversion is an essential good of the church) but to witness and to learn. The serious attempt to enrich the Christian spiritual tradition with the spiritual wisdom of Islam or Buddhism or Hinduism is well in place. Indeed, we could say that one of the highest levels of dialogue in the world today are those attempts by mature and formed men and women to pray and listen together across the spiritual traditions of the world. Like the mature Thomas Merton in Asia, there are many who come to those places not as preachers but as pilgrims and learners.

But, it might be asked, what does this have to do with the average person who has no contact with either non-Occidental lands or other religious traditions? How do those movements touch them?

To that question—and it is a fair one—a number of points could be made. At the most general level, we need to remind ourselves that the church is both a *learner* and a teacher (*ecclesia discens et docens*, as the Latin aphorism would have it). This is a very old notion in the church, but it is only now that we have had the perspective to emphasize the *learning* aspect. What the church constantly must learn is how better to be both a faithful witness to and preacher of the mystery of salvation which comes to us from God in Jesus Christ. Every movement that enlarges our perspective on the Gospel is, in itself, an instrument of greater fidelity to the Gospel. Thus, at this level, if Buddhism reminds us of the need for compassion or the Hindu teaches us about renunciation or the Muslim exemplifies greater submission to the awe-ful majesty of God, we must be willing learners not so that we can become Buddhists or Hindus or Muslims but because we can become more authentically Catholic. A decade before Vatican II Bede Griffiths put the matter directly in his autobiographical memoir *The Golden String:*

> For centuries now Christianity has developed in a westerly direction taking on an ever more western character of thought and expression. If it is ever to penetrate deeply into the East it will have to find a more easterly form, in which the genius of the peoples of the East will be able to find expression. For Christianity will never realize its full stature as a genuine Catholicism, until it has incorporated into itself all that is valid and true in all the different religious traditions.

What every Christian must learn is that to be a learner is to adopt a stance of humility: to admit that not everything we do or say is the final word or the final gesture. Humility, to employ that much overused word, is openness. To be a learner involves certain risks. After all, not everything we have learned is good. There is also the danger that we can run after fads and become entranced by the fashions of the day. This is a particular temptation in the area of spirituality where anyone with two summer Institutes under his belt can become a self-described "spiritual director."

It has been the particular merit of the Notre Dame theologian John Dunne that he has spelled out, in a series of books, how one can "pass over" or "cross over" into other traditions and/or cultures in order to "return" or "come home" again enriched and deepened by those experiences. Dunne does not tout a form of spiritual tourism by which one inspects the poor or observes the Hindus or encounters places to return with a bag full of spiritual snapshots. He encourages his readers to journey with both one's own faith and one's willingness to learn in order to deepen and expand one's sense of journey toward God. As one reads through Dunne's works it is clear that he has started with the trajectory of the self and its finitude ("I am and I will die") to enlarge that trajectory outside of the self toward a consideration of myself as part of the larger reality of the world.

John Dunne's project of crossing over and returning is not as exotic as one would think at first glance. Although his writings are dense with meaning and graceful in style, there is a sense in which Dunne's thought parallels an old truth in the Catholic spiritual tradition: to bring to prayerful awareness the things we encounter in our lives. In other words, in the best sense of the term, we "politicize" our prayer to the degree that prayer is energized by all of the circumstances we encounter as we "cross over" into the world of the mundane and the ordinary as well as the world of the exotic and unfamiliar.

The great challenge of our time, of course, is ever to expand that world of the ordinary so that it enriches our prayer life in constant and, perhaps, radical ways. It is, in fact, an openness to the ordinary seen through the eyes of faith that can become the graced moment—the *kairos* for a deeper and fuller conversion.

The history of the Christian tradition testifies to the truth of this fact. In his *Testament*, Saint Francis of Assisi marks his conversion to the time when he was able to look at lepers and not recoil from the sight of them. Mother Teresa of Calcutta marks the beginnings of her extraordinary apostolate to the destitute poor to the day when, after years in the convent, she looked out of a train window and saw—really *saw*—for the first time, the teeming masses of poor in India. Oscar Romero was a conventionally pious priest until he began to realize what it really meant to be a poor *campesino* in his native El Salvador. Thomas Merton had been a professed monk and a priest for well over a decade when, in a famous scene described in *Conjectures of a Guilty Bystander* (1966) he went to Louisville one day and in the midst of the city suddenly became aware of his immense love for the people swirling about him; it was, as he wrote, like "walking from a dream of separateness."

What is extraordinary about all of those incidents—and the examples could be multiplied—is their homeliness. These things happened not as theophanies on mountaintops but in the hillside of Umbria or on a train in India or, in Merton's words, at "the corner of Fourth and Walnut." Nor need they be understood only as "twice-born" experiences by which people were converted to new, more radical forms of religious living. They were undoubtedly that but—and this is the crucial point—they also were axial moments in the life of prayer.

In each of these instances what occurred to the recipients was a kind of healing of the chasm of what they did and how they prayed. There was, in other words, a kind of reintegration of the person so they became, simultaneously, doers and pray-ers. The ordinary became for them extraordinary and, in the process, their prayer become political—it was for the *polis*.

There is something very Catholic (but, to be sure, not exclusively Catholic) about this: seeing the ordinary as a sign of God's invitation and graciousness. That is why there has always been a steady stream in Catholic spirituality that insists on sanctifying the ordinary; of seeing all of creation as sacramental not in some vague romantic sense but in the close proximity of ordinary life; a life very much like that of Jesus who preached *Abba* love to (and with) the poor, the blind, the heretical, the marginal, and the naturally unlovely.

Earlier in this chapter we spoke of prayer as moving out in concentric circles from the local and the immediate to that which is more universal, which is to say, Catholic. We do not want that image to be conceived of as in radical opposition to the traditional images of prayer as ascent of the ladder or the higher reaches of the mountaintop. Those images carry with them the sanction of traditionally valid insights. What we need to recall is that transcendence carries the meaning of ascent and of to cross over; we speak of transcendence and not merely ascendance.

We need to climb up (and away) from the imperious demands of the self as ego not to abolish the self but to make it open to God, who stands across not only us but everything and everyone who is in the world. To seek that which is transcendent is not to abolish the self but to complete it. And the self, let us remind ourselves, does not exist as an ethereal abstraction ripped from either the body in particular or bodily history in general. The self—and there is really no paradox here, simply an empirical fact—is meaningless without reference to the fact that it is a social self. Even the most cloistered Carthusian would affirm that he prays not only for his salvation but for the good of the church.

John Cassian, in one of his monastic conferences, tells of a desert ascetic named Hero who was so severe in his monastic discipline that he refused to join his fellow monks for dinner on Easter Sunday. Cassian says that an angel of Satan tempted him to throw himself headlong down a well with a promise that, because of his merits, no harm would come to him. Hero was pulled out half dead, but two days later he died still clinging to his illusion. Only with difficulty, Cassian reports, did the monks decide not to classify him a suicide.

Cassian's homely *exemplum* carries with it a profound truth. Hero's fifty years in the desert failed to teach him the important truth that his prayer had to be political and not solely personal. We could add: By failing to be political, Hero's prayer could never be considered Catholic.

A Prayer

One by one, Lord, I see and love all those whom you have given me to sustain and charm my life.

One by one I also number all those who make up that other beloved family which has gradually surrounded me, its unity fashioned out of the most disparate elements with affinities of the heart, of scientific research, and of thought.

And again one by one—more vaguely it is true, yet all-inclusively—I call before me the whole vast anonymous army of living humanity; those who surround me and support me though I do not know them; those who come and those who go; above all, those who in office, laboratory, and factory, through their vision of truth or despite their error, truly believe in the progress of earthly reality and who today will take up again their impassioned pursuit of the light.

This restless multitude, confused or orderly, the immensity of which terrifies us; this ocean of humanity whose slow, monotonous wave-flows troubles the hearts even of those whose faith is most firm: it is to this deep that I thus desire all the fibers of my being should respond.

All the things in the world to which this day will bring increase; all those will diminish; all those too that will die; all of them, Lord, I try to gather into my arms, so as to hold them out to you in offering.

This is the material of my sacrifice; the only material you desire.

This prayer, part of *The Mass on the World*, was composed by Teilhard de Chardin, the French Jesuit scientist and mystic. Beginning with his years as a soldier in World War One, Teilhard worked out a long prayer that was a sort of mystical substitute to be used when he was unable to celebrate Mass. He worked over this idea (and its wording) for years afterward and it became, during his years in the Far East, his way of being faithful to the priestly function when he was unable actually to participate in the eucharistic liturgy.

Based on an analogy with the doctrine of eucharistic transubstantiation, Teilhard conceived of himself as saying "words of consecration" over the reality of the cosmos and its inhabitants so as to transform and offer the cosmos, saved by Christ, to the Father in adoration. Teilhard's theology emphasized both the creation of the world through the Word and its redemption through that same Word. It is a theology that is both strongly Johannine (think of the prologue to the Fourth Gospel) and Pauline in its inspiration. Teilhard's vision, strongly mystical and equally original, reflects the utter seriousness of the presence of Christ in the world as he suffuses everything that *is*.

Teilhard meditated throughout his life on the concentric nature of Christ's presence (he used the language of *spheres*) to insist that the brute world of matter, consciousness, humanity, and a Future Not Yet Realized was all part of the Christian world view. He was a political thinker, but his politics did not rest with human relations; it was a politics of the cosmos.

I have excerpted this prayer from Teilhard's *The Heart of Matter*, translated by René Hague (New York: Harcourt, Brace, and Javonovich, 1978), p. 120.

A Note on Readings

Karl Rahner's essay "Toward a Fundamental Theological Interpretation of Vatican II," was published in *Theological Studies* 40 (1979), pp. 716–27, and reprinted in *Vatican II: The Unfinished Agenda*, edited by Lucien Richard et al. (Mahwah, NJ: Paulist, 1987), with a number of other essays reflecting Rahner's basic ecclesiological concerns. The essay can also be found in Rahner's *Theological Investigations* 20 (New York: Crossroad, 1981), pp. 77–89.

Walbert Buhlmann's *The Coming of the Third Church* (Maryknoll, NY: Orbis, 1977) has been very influential in arguing for a post-European church.

The most thorough investigation of the notion of Catholicity is Avery Dulles's *The Catholicity of the Church* (Oxford: Clarendon Press, 1985). The book has abundant notes and a bibliography. It is an excellent work to read to see how Catholic prayer must be, in the deep sense of the term, political prayer.

For a good treatment of sacramental worship in a political perspective, see Michael Downey, *Clothed in Christ: The Sacraments and Christian Living* (New York: Crossroad, 1987).

My information on Janusz Korczak comes from Betty Jean Lifton's *The King of Children: A Biography of Janusz Korczak* (New York: Farrar, Straus, and Giroux, 1988).

I was much indebted in this chapter to Francis Schüssler Fiorenza's *Foundational Theology: Jesus and the Church* (New York: Crossroad, 1984). Another fine work on the changing character of theology with respect to the church in the world is *The Reception of Vatican II*, edited by Giuseppe Alberigo et al. (Washington, DC: Catholic University of America Press, 1987).

Bede Griffiths's autobiography, *The Golden String*, first published in 1954, has been recently reprinted (Springfield, IL: Templegate, 1980).

John Dunne has produced a steady stream of works since the early 1970s. For this chapter I made most use of three of his more recent books: *The Reasons of the Heart* (Notre Dame, IN: University of Notre Dame Press, 1978), *The Church of the Poor Devil* (New York: Macmillan, 1982), and *The House of Wisdom* (San Francisco: Harper and Row, 1985). For an excellent survey of Dunne's method, see Jon Nilson, "Doing Theology by Heart: John S. Dunne's Theological Method," *Theological Studies* 48 (1987), pp. 65–86.

A partial collection of Cassian's conferences can be found in *John Cassian: Conferences*, translated with a preface by Colm Luibheid (Mahwah, NJ: Paulist, 1985).

9

STAGES

A stream of pilgrims answering the bell
Trailed up the steps as I went down them
Towards the bottle-green, still
shade of an oak.

Seamus Heaney, Station Island

In the Christian tradition there is a persistent theme of understanding the life of prayer and Christian perfection as a series of steps or levels by which a person changes from a life of sin or carnality to a life of Christian perfection. That there are stages or steps is a constant; what those stages and steps are is subject to a wide variety of interpretation and description. Saint Benedict, for example, in his *Rule*, lists twelve steps (*gradus*) of humility by which a monk learns to perfect himself as a monk but, it should be noted, Benedict elaborates an earlier schema from John Cassian who describes ten steps. John Climacus, a seventh-century monk, is famous for a book (*The Ladder of Divine Love*) describing thirty steps in the perfection of a monk; it is a work of such authority that it is read *in toto* each year during Lent in Orthodox monasteries. Walter Hilton, the fourteenth-century English mystic, would take up the same image (but with much less of a schematic apparatus) in his much-loved work *The Ladder [or Scale] of Perfection*, where there are two steps of advancement separated by a dark period of desolation and purgation.

Written in the Middle Ages, Saint Bonaventure's *Itinerarium* combines the mysticism of Francis and his own Augustinian desire for self-scrutiny to chart out the soul's ascent to God, which he sees as happening in six stages (corresponding to the days of creation) with a final stage of rest in God after the manner of the Sabbath. This seven-stage journey may well have inspired Dante as he made his own way in the *Divine Comedy.* Saint Teresa of Avila uses the imagery of a castle (*The Interior Castle*) with seven mansions, while her fellow Carmelite mystic, Saint John of the Cross, describes the mystic journey as the ascent of a mountain—the Mt. Carmel which was the supposed place in the Holy Land where the Carmelite order was founded. Earlier, the author of the *Cloud of Unknowing,* drawing on a tradition that goes back to the patristic writer, Saint Gregory of Nyssa, also sees the ascent of prayer as a climb up the mountain (in this case, Sinai) to enter into the cloud that Moses experienced at the giving of the Law.

One common description of the stages of prayer to which we have already alluded is the passage from the way of purgation to the way of illumination to the final stage of union (*via unitiva*) with God. This is a very old notion in Christian spirituality, with roots that go at least as far back as Plotinus, which one still finds discussed in the mystical literature today. This triple ascent is, as it were, a distillation of the entire ascent literature in Christian spirituality. In our own century it was Jacques Maritain who gave a philosophical-theological account of this upward path of knowing in his classic treatise *The Degrees of Knowledge* (ET:1959).

It would be far too complicated to comment on these various schemas of spiritual development, but it is possible to make two generalizations that shed light on the notion of grades of spiritual growth.

In the first instance, we should note that the idea of growth, by stages, in spiritual development is a very widespread and ancient one. All of the great religious traditions of the world possess a mystical tradition that sees union with the Ultimate (however differently it may be conceived) as a gradual path by which one first masters the self and then, in consequence, becomes open to the Ultimate. The ways in which this may be accomplished differ from one tradition to another, but the notion of the spiritual path—usually described as upward (even when, as in the Eastern traditions, it is also inward)—is a constant. All traditions, furthermore, have at least two stages: the turning from the self (or the false self) and the turning to the Ultimate conceived, variously, as the True Self or the Non-Self or to the Transcendent Other.

The seemingly complicated tradition of stages becomes less complicated when we reflect that outside of the purely religious tradition there is an almost universal belief in growth by stages for the human person as he or she matures physically, intellectually, and psychologically. The anthropological study of rites of passage (made famous by the classic study of Arnold van Gennep) indicates quite clearly that there is a deep acceptance of the notion that people pass through grades (e.g., from childhood to young manhood or womanhood) in their life which have enough significance to be noted with sacred ceremonies involving the motifs of death/rebirth, new knowledge, etc. Even in our less-sacralized world we have seen highly influential scholars (e.g., Piaget, Erikson, etc.) who have tracked the developmental growth of children through stages that are marked by intellectual/physical growth as well as by growth in the acceptance of values and ethics. Students of religion will remember that Baron von Hugel uses the typological schema of growth from childhood to adulthood as the starting point of his great study on prayer and mysticism, *The Mystical Element in Religion*. What one finds, in short, is the notion of advancement, growth, maturity, and/or development in human life.

What Hugel has suggested as a student of spiritual growth has been worked out from the perspective of the development of faith itself by such scholars as James Fowler. Fowler's influential book *Stages of Faith: The Psychology of Human Development and Quest for Meaning* (1981) has attempted to chart out the deepening of religious faith from that primordial basic trust of the infant (posited by, among others, Erik Erikson) to the fully mature faith of the converted adult. Fowler's work has received wide comment; its implications for a theory of the spiritual life is patent, even though Fowler himself does not spend a good deal of his energy thinking through the kinds of prayer/devotion appropriate to each of his seven stages of faith-development that he provides in his analysis. It is not difficult, however, to extrapolate what such prayer would look like in its main form were one to juxtapose prayer to Fowler's stages.

Secondly, the description of the stages of growth tend to employ images that express the requirement of human effort and human pain (the climbing of the mountain, the penetration of the castle, the ascent of the ladder) with the concomitant death of—depending on the schema—the false self, the habits of sin, the comforts of custom, etc. Saint Paul understood and expressed it in some of his more elegant formulations: putting off the things of childhood for the life of an adult, the transition from the carnal person to the spiritual person, etc. The key text in Paul for this growth is his famous observation to the church at Corinth: "When I was a child, I spoke like a child, I reasoned like a child; when I became a man [i.e., an adult] I gave up childish ways" (1 Cor. 13:11). Even human growth, quite apart from the religious dimension, carries with it a certain arduousness and challenge as any parent who has seen a child move into adolescence can attest.

Leaving aside the particular formulations of the stages, there is one thing that is very clear about all of them, and it is this: The stages in the spiritual life mark a change in consciousness or, to use another phrase popular today, a shift in horizon. When Søren Kierkegaard, for instance, charted human growth from the aesthetic to the ethical to the religious mode of life, he was not talking about something that evolved naturally like biological growth and maturity. The move from the aesthetic plane to the ethical consists in the conscious act of the will to move from a life of pure sensation to a life of duty and obligation. It is the move of one who is an outlaw to one who affirms the need for rights and obligations. Each transition, in short, means a moment of conscious decision. I leave aside the issue of how grace works in this schema; it is assumed both by Kierkegaard and myself.

From that level to the religious one involved, at least as Kierkegaard understood it, a "leap" from the rationality of

ethics to pure faith in God. For Kierkegaard, the paradigm of
the religious person is Abraham—the Kierkegaardian "Knight
of Faith"—who would even suspend his respect for the law to
sacrifice his son Isaac because this was demanded as a pure
act of faith by God.

I use Kierkegaard because his formulation is so well known.
Any of the other descriptive accounts of religious stages
would do as well to make the basic points that I want to
make:

- Religious stages involve the will to move from one step to
another even when, as in Catholic accounts, the will is predis-
posed and moved by the free gift of God which is grace. The
ascent, in other words, does not occur by sheer acts of determi-
nation alone.
- These steps involve some kind of knowing.
- This knowing, to be understood in the broadest sense of
the term, brings about a larger sense of perspective—a broader
horizon of possibilities and responsibilities.
- This enlargement is never complete. It is not as if one
reaches a plateau of growth in perfection. It is not false mod-
esty when the great mystics describe themselves as beginners
in the spiritual life or great sinners. Such proclamations suggest that they, better than most, more fully understand that
the broad horizon against which they grow is the infinite horizon of the Absolute which is, of course, God in all of his mystery and depth. There is no mystic with whom I am familiar
who has said that the journey has ended or the goal reached.
Each experience of union deepens the need and hunger for
union yet again.

My suspicion is that many "ordinary folks" are a bit put off
by much of the vocabulary and imagery of spiritual development. Most of us find the notion of scaling Mt. Carmel or
ascending the mystical path as a dauntingly elitist exercise
more suitable for the Carthusian than the suburbanite. It has
not helped my own sense of these matters to remember those
icons (not that rare in the iconic tradition) of monks, prelates,
and hierarchs climbing a ladder toward heaven only to reach
the lower and middle rungs and to find themselves falling off

headlong toward waiting devils at the open maw of hell. The first time I saw one of those pictures I thought it would be a lot safer to hang around the foot of the ladder rather than attempt the ascent.

There is the further problem that many people find the very notion of the individual soul finding a solitary path toward God too individualistic and too detached from the incarnational aspect(s) of Christianity. Many have objected to contemplative monasticism on these very grounds arguing— wrongly, by the bye—that such a tradition has more in common with the pagan Plotinus than it does with the Gospels. Later in this chapter we will argue that a genuine sense of spiritual growth must take into account the social character of such growth. We will not argue for a Plotinian *Solus cum Solo* ("Alone with the Alone"), although, as is obvious, spiritual growth must have a strong component of personal decision in it if it is to have meaning at all. To deny that is to affirm the crudest form of determinism.

If, however, we take seriously the twin facts that everyone is called to the life of prayer in the church and that the tradition of prayer speaks variously of the ascent by stages, then it follows that there must be some way in which we can understand this tradition in less-forbidding ways while, at the same time, remaining faithful to the tradition and its biblical roots.

To "demystify" or "deconstruct" this tradition we might well think of the stages of the spiritual life not in terms of steps or grades but, in a far simpler language, of Christian conversion—of what the New Testament calls, simply, *metanoia*. This would be a language that would emphasize different ways of living as opposed to different stages of ascent.

By conversion, in this discussion, we do not mean those rapid transformations of blinding grace by which a Saul of Tarsus becomes a Paul, the apostle to the Gentiles, but rather that *process* by which we turn from one way of life toward a new and different way. Conversion is that response which we give to the cry with which Jesus began his public preaching: "The time is fulfilled, and the kingdom of God is at hand. Repent and believe in the gospel!" (Mark 1:15).

The term "conversion" is capable of various translations into English: repentance, change of mind, change of heart, or conversion itself. When Jesus speaks of repentance in the above verse, he was using a word that had a long history behind it. Conversion in the Hebrew experience meant a change by which people left off their old ways in order to live in greater fidelity to Jahweh and the covenant between Jahweh and the people of Israel. Furthermore, let me again emphasize, the notion of conversion carries with it the sense of something that is ongoing; "be converted" carries with it the notion of "be continually in a state of conversion." At its base, it means giving up one way of life for a different one. As we know from a reading of the prophetic literature, the urgent message of the prophets was essentially a *continual* call for a return to convenental fidelity.

In what does this conversion consist?

Metanoia (the Greek word in the Gospels that means conversion) contains within it a twofold dynamic—what the scholastic tradition calls *aversio* (turning from) and *conversio* (turning toward). We might say a few words about each.

Aversion to sin is the first step in the dynamics of conversion. Fully understood, aversion to sin does not mean "giving up" this act or getting away from some significant omission in one's life. It means, rather—as the word itself indicates—a turning of the back on a certain kind of life. It means, in short, to see one's life so holistically that it becomes possible to say that it is, as currently lived, skewed, eccentric, deformed, and without a full sense of purpose. It is when we come to this realization that it is possible to say that we want to reject it, and in this rejection, the actions or omissions that flow from it cease to be options for us even if this process of "ceasing" takes time and effort.

It is helpful, in this regard, to remember that the verb "to sin" can also be translated as "to miss the mark." Sin, then, should be understood not as a breaking of a rule but as a fundamentally flawed orientation. To be a sinner means that the trajectory of our life is out of line or wide of the mark or not on target. Aversion, then, is a turning from that errant trajectory toward a truer one.

An example, even a trite one, might help make the point. A spouse may come to the clear light of awareness one day in which he or she sees his role as spouse as hopelessly inadequate: a tissue of selfishness, neglect, self-centered preoccupation in favor of the gratification of career or pleasure or whatever. When such a spouse turns away from (*aversio*) such a way of being, the acts which flow from that state also begin to recede. True aversion comes, then, not when one says "I must pay more attention to my family" but when one sees that a chosen lifestyle is the root of inattention. The success of Alcoholics Anonymous—to use another example—derives from the demand that one not say "I will not drink" but from the statement "I am an alcoholic." When one states that existential fact, it follows, if one experiences *aversio*, that "I will not drink." Acts, after all, derive from a certain human disposition and not vice versa.

This is a point worth underscoring because it helps us to get an authentic sense of the first part of conversion, which is the turning away from a former kind of life. "Getting converted" is so much a part of the patois of fundamentalism (my native parts are filled with signs tacked to pine trees with the imperative message: REPENT!) that we can trivialize the idea into pleas to give up, in the immortal words of the country song, "cigarettes and whiskey and wild, wild women." We might do well to abstain from the same but conversion means the deeper sense of understanding the answer to the fundamental question of existence: "Who are we?" and, following on that, "What would we or should we like to be?"

If *aversio* is an existential experience, it follows that we must then pursue its dynamic further to ask what replaces that aversion once we no longer wish to live the way we have lived before. As we turn from one way of life we then must turn to another way. Obviously, this can mean something that is not specifically religious. We might make a moral conversion (away from theft to honesty) or a social one (away from the carefree pleasures of youth to the responsibilities of family and occupation) or simply a conversion toward survival (away from drugs to a life of freedom from chemical dependency) or culture (from ignorance to education). These are all moral conversions broadly understood. Such conversions may or may not have a religious component to them.

Religious conversion, however, means to move away from a preoccupation or fixation on the finite which defines our life in a manner that makes it impossible to reach out to God. In fact, we might define sin in this way—as a style of life that so fixes itself on finite gratification that one cannot fix on God. Note, we are not denying the goodness of finite gratification (gratifications are a great gift from God; they are the source of the joy which comes from being human) but a short-sighted fixation on them. To be converted religiously means, in essence, to convert to that full human freedom in which it becomes possible to know and love infinitely. The capacity to love more is to affirm that openness of love which finds its ultimate meaning in the belief that love is infinite. To love self, spouse, family, friends, and so on, is to taste the love of God. What is radical in the message of Jesus is his conviction and teaching that to dare love that which is not naturally lovely is to imitate fully *Abba:* "For if you love those who love you, what reward have you? Do not even the tax collectors do the same? And if you salute only your brethren, what more are you doing than others? Do not even the Gentiles do the same? You therefore must be perfect as the heavenly Father is perfect" (Matt. 5:46–48).

There is one other aspect of religious conversion that needs to be noted. It is so easy to think of such conversion(s) in the abstract that we need to remind ourselves that the moments of conversion happen to a person while they are going through the simultaneous process of developing as a human person. People, in short, grow up. Religious conversions, then, must be seen in the light of human development. Put concretely, it means that the process of aversion/conversion is going to look differently when we think of adolescent needs or the condition of being old. The reception of the Gospel as a livable reality must be understood in terms of the life cycle of the person as he or she grows socially, culturally, intellectually, and so on.

It takes no sustained thought to see the basic truth of this. My primary-school daughter "receives" religious images in a far different way than I do. As I have argued in *Faith Rediscovered* (1987) adults who have (or purport to have) a crisis of faith, in fact, often experience a clash between adult values and a kind of "Sunday school" understanding of what faith and/or the teachings of faith are all about. They have matured in many ways but still have, at best, an immature or underdeveloped notion of the data of their faith. It is only natural that they should resist that immature faith just as they leave off the other activities of a childhood that now should recede into fond memory. Their rebellion is not against God but against an immature notion of God which may be, in its own right, purificatory and helpful.

This is hardly an original insight. A good deal of Andrew Greeley's sociological research has devoted itself to the correlation between the growth of the life cycle and its needs/reactions to the story of faith as it is encountered in the proclamation of the church. Greeley's books over the last fifteen years or so have hammered away at the thesis that we must recognize a correlation between our own personal story and the story which the church tells of Jesus the Christ. The obvious truth that Greeley advances is that the story which is told ought to be commensurate with the human growth of the life-cycle process itself. Furthermore, there is strong empirical evidence that young people who leave off the practice of faith tend to return to it at those moments in the life cycle when the need for reintegration into adult society are strongest: at marriage, when a child is born, and, interestingly enough, when one's own child enters school.

What one sees from a number of different disciplines is that there are moments in life when one makes religious choices and advances which seem to unfold as the life process itself unfolds. When we cut through the specialized language of the theologian or the sociologist or psychologist what is seen is something that can rightfully be called a process of conversion: a turning from one way of life and a turning toward another way.

The fullest study of conversion in English is Walter Conn's *Christian Conversion: A Developmental Interpretation of Autonomy and Surrender* (1986). Combining theological reflection, philosophical analysis, and developmental psychology, Conn sets out a sophisticated account of the relationship of religious conversion to the development of the individual. Without attempting to rehearse the main lines of this persuasively detailed analysis, we can satisfy ourselves with his major conclusions. Conn argues that true Christian conversion is an adult phenomenon (those conversions by which adolescents overcome "identity crises" are moral conversions) by which a person becomes capable of Christian living. Conn writes (he is using Thomas Merton as his "test case"):

> The personal measure of Christian living, therefore, is the conscience which has experienced a Christian conversion at once cognitive, affective, moral, and religious. Only a person thus converted is fully and concretely sensitive to the loving life of Jesus. In Merton's life we discovered again the fundamental Gospel truth that lies at the heart of the Christian tradition: the radical religious conversion of Christian conscience finds its fullest realization in loving compassion—the self-transcending perfection of human empathy and justice. In its total surrender such religious conversion radically relativizes the moral autonomy of Christian conscience.

But what does this all have to do with the issue of prayer?

The first, and most obvious, thing is that the very process of conversion itself can be seen in the light of what we have argued in the opening chapter, i.e., that the dynamics of conversion can be seen as prayer itself. The basis for that statement can be found in the fact that in the dynamic of turning from and turning to relationship is affirmed. We could not turn to without at least an implicit awareness that there is someone toward whom we can make the turn. Every conversion to God is an exercise (or a reinforcement) of that fundamental option by which we orient our lives as a whole away from sin and toward the infinite horizon which is God.

The converse, of course, is equally true. Every time we pray we undergo a conversion or, to say it better: Every time we pray we affirm our state of being converted, since the very act of prayer involves a habitual or conscious decision to turn to God in an explicit manner. Prayer, then, is conversion worked out in the concrete every time we pray and articulated and celebrated by the use of language, gesture, worship, and so on.

Secondly, when we think of the dual movement of turning from and turning toward we see that, at the root, conversion, like prayer, involves at the very least two stages, stages which can be equated with purgation and union. Purgation stands, in this instance, as the willingness to turn from complete autonomy and the limits of finite self-gratification, while union is the shorthand way of describing the willingness to stand in relationship to that ultimate mystery which is God.

A useful metaphor to illustrate this is the call of the disciples in the Gospels: "And Jesus said to them, 'Follow me and I will make you fishers of men.' And immediately they left their nets and followed him" (Mark 1:17–18; for a more theological rendering of these calls, see John 1:35ff.). What we see in that scene is a giving up of one way of life (fishing) for another (discipleship) triggered by an invitation and a response. The twin actions of old life/new life and call/response sums up economically the planes of conversion and prayer.

The value of linking conversion and prayer as a way of understanding, at least at the basic level, the stages of prayer is that it helps us remove the notion of stages as an elitist ascent. The stages of prayer, in short, are nothing more than the basic steps by which a person moves from being a nonbeliever into a believer.

Seen in that fashion, the elaborations of the spiritual writers who have charted these stages in particular detail can be seen as nothing more than the attempt to sort out and specify that which is, at base, the simple Gospel demand that we repent and be converted to the Reign of God. They are descriptive blaze marks of the path of greater conversion, or psychological accounts of how the process of conversion actually unfolds in this or that person's experience of the Christian life. They are *not* normative. The Christian need not ascend, lock step, up the thirty rungs of John Climacus's ladder. The description of the rungs may well be, however, helpful analyses of how conversion works out in concrete circumstances. They also give us a precious insight into the workings of the prayer life of our most conspicuous masters and mistresses of the spiritual life.

If Conn is correct in seeing Christian conversion as something that happens in maturity—and I think he is right—it also follows that Christian prayer refines itself in the conversion process until it also becomes mature. At a certain level, this is a truism. People may start off in the life of prayer "imagining" it to be a kind of conversion carried on with a Someone who is larger than life. We might even imagine that Someone as looking like a person writ large, e.g., the patriarchal figure of artistic depiction. To say that such an image is an immature one is to miss the far more important point that its very immaturity, unless it is overcome, carries with it a lethal virus of alienation and disbelief. If that Someone does not answer my prayer at a time when an answer is desperately desired ("please heal my injured child"), that Someone seems capricious or indifferent or cruel. At any rate, the conversation seems over. After all, we might reason, if I were that Someone I could not let a child like that suffer. Both Dostoevsky in *The Brothers Karamazov* and Albert Camus in *The Plague* wrestled with that very issue. That same sense of immaturity, it seems to me, is at the heart of Sigmund Freud's withering dismissal of religious faith in *The Future of an Illusion*.

What the Christian tradition of prayer insists upon is that when we confront God in prayer our notion of God undergoes a deepening sense of mystery precisely as we mature in prayer. The mystics are hardly Pollyannas about the disappointments inherent in life. What John of the Cross learned in his cramped prison cell was that God's seeming absence was, in fact, presence. In learning that John refined both his theology of prayer as well as his sense of the reality of God. Likewise, Julian in her anchorhold could affirm, in her illness, words that Eliot would use centuries later: "all things are well / and all manner of things are well."

This gradual (gradual—from *gradus*—step/stage) maturing of the process of prayer helps us to understand what is behind the many categorizations of the stages of the interior life. They can be understood as insights into spiritual maturity.

Obviously, this maturation need not be understood only in terms of an ascent. Indeed, it may even be more helpful to understand this process in other ways. Elsewhere in this book I have suggested the image of concentric circles radiating out into an ever more deepening experience of prayer as universal (catholic).

Another image that has the warrant of use from the Second Vatican Council is worth some extended comment: the life of prayer/conversion considered as pilgrimage.

Pilgrimage, as I have argued in *The Catholic Heritage* is an ancient religious phenomenon in Catholic Christianity and has also served as a metaphor for the spiritual journey of the Christian. It is the image to which Dante makes reference throughout the *Commedia* and to which he appeals (in the last canto of the *Paradiso*) to explain his journey. The rigors of pilgrimage (remember that it was both a devotional and *penitential* practice in the church) are hard to recover in an age when pilgrimages can be arranged by a travel agency and taken in air-conditioned comfort. Modern-day pilgrimages, by and large, require little penance beyond the rigors of airline food and the tackiness of tourist hotels. What we must imagine (the Wife of Bath, Chaucer tells us, made this trip) is walking from England to Venice, taking a boat to Haifa, walking to Jerusalem, and then making the return trip without decent roads, hotels, secure sources of foodstuffs, little police protection, barbarous medicine, no modern communications, etc.

A pilgrimage was not a weekend ramble. It was a rigorous journey that had the following characteristics worth emphasizing: (a) It was arduous; (b) it had a goal that was specific; (c) it was done with a religious motive and its final destination was religious; (d) it was normally done in company, i.e., it had a social dimension.

That the above is a useful metaphor for the Christian life seems obvious. Every Christian, prelate and peasant, walks toward the eschaton. That journey is an arduous one, but everyone who takes it is sustained by the conviction that there is a goal ahead of us that is the object of the journey as well as the power that pulls us forward. The many decisions to keep going as well as resistance to the temptation to quit walking are the twin elements which make up, simultaneously, our process of conversion and our life of prayer. To make the pilgrimage is to affirm the worthiness of the goal. The rigor of the passage is alleviated by the encouragement and example of our fellow pilgrims. Walter Hilton, writing when the pilgrimage journey was still a possibility (he died in 1396, four years before his compatriot, Geoffrey Chaucer), catches the idea perfectly in the *Ladder of Perfection:*

> ... if you wish to be a spiritual pilgrim, you must divest yourself of all you possess; that is of deeds both bad and good, and leave them all behind you. Recognize your own poverty, so that you will not place your confidence in any good work; instead, always be desiring the grace of deeper love, and seeking the spiritual presence of Jesus. If you do this, you will be setting your heart wholly on reaching Jerusalem, and on nothing else. In other words, set your heart wholly on obtaining the love of Jesus and whatever spiritual vision of himself that he is willing to grant, for it is to this end alone that you have been created and redeemed; that is your beginning and your end; your joy and your bliss. Therefore, whatever you may possess, and however fruitful your activities, regard them all as worthless without the inward certainty and experience of this love. Keep this intention constantly in mind and hold it firmly; it will sustain you among the perils of your pilgrimage.

If there is a weakness in Hilton's rendering of the pilgrim motif it is that it focuses exclusively on the individual pilgrim and pays little attention to the company of pilgrims which is the church, the pilgrim people of God.

We want to emphasize that the conversion process understood as a maturation of Christian living is done in the context of the worshiping community. We convert *in* the church and *through* our participation in its life. How?

The framework of this maturation process is found in the participation of the church's sacramental life. After all, it is a commonplace that the sacraments track our growth as individuals. We have traditionally understood baptism as the sacrament of initiation that is complemented by the sacrament of maturation, which is the reception of the Holy Spirit in confirmation. Ongoing participation in the sacrament of the Body and Blood of Christ is seen as the sustaining force of our pilgrim's journey; eight centuries ago Saint Thomas Aquinas called it the "food of pilgrims" (*esca viatorum*) which is the foretaste of the pilgrimage goal. Penance reconciles us to God and the community of believers as an outward sign of our need for continual conversion. Marriage and orders are rites of passage appropriate to particular ages and needs, just as the anointing of the sick is a healing presence at times of crisis and, preeminently, in that transition from pilgrimage to being in the Lord.

Hearing God's word is an ongoing part of this maturing process as we attempt to come again to listen and respond to that which the church proclaims across time and space. Our capacity to receive this word should mature as we move from understanding this preached word in terms of moralism to terms of love, compassion, and yearning.

The deepest sense of maturity comes as gradually (i.e., by stages) we become more Catholic. "More Catholic" does not mean more attached to the church as a visible reality—it is not our business to be converted *to* the church—but in our ability to pray more universally, to shift our horizon from where we are in the local community to the needs and hopes of all communities, to enlarge our vision to the whole rather than a preoccupation with the particular. It is, to go back to the image we employed before, to see our lives as Catholics as a series of radiating circles by which we move from where we are to a Catholic sense of our solidarity with all who are in Christ either in fact or by right. We convert, in short, in the church, and through our conversion the church itself is also converted.

A curious paradox occurs as we mature through the ongoing process of conversion and prayer. The life of faith becomes riskier and more demanding in terms of real faith. When we are very young it is easy to be certain and satisfied in that certainty. When I was twenty I had all the answers. Thirty years later I think that I am now beginning to see clearly what the questions are. The very process of maturation brings with it the sloughing off of easily held verities to the

far more treacherous plane of deepening our faith in the existence of verities. That growth in maturity indicates that the
way of purgation is open-ended and not merely to be construed as the first step on the spiritual ladder.

Without overdramatizing the situation we can say that the
dark night or the dark cloud or the desolations of which the
mystics speak is nothing more than the letting go of those
easy truths in order to live more nakedly in Truth. This
should not discourage us. In fact, it would seem an inevitable
consequence of growing up and becoming older. Only the
most blindered fail to see that human projects (even those in
the church among the people of God) are limited and short of
perfection. Only the most self-satisfied fail to note how difficult it is to overcome the inertia of habit and rut in our lives.
Only the most smug of us can live life without a twinge of
regret at the opportunities we have missed or the paths not
taken. In fact, it is probably truer to reality to say that those
who do not experience some difficulty in their spiritual lives
escape such moments more from their complacency than
from the simplicity of their faith.

Such difficulties in our life as Christians simply mirror
our own pilgrimages in life toward old age and death. Things
we could do once with ease we now do with difficulty. The
body shows its age and does not respond in the same way.
People grow away from us and friends age and die. How we
respond to this says a great deal about how we view life and
how we have lived. It also tells us how we face the prospect of
death. We must come face to face with our regrets and our
satisfactions.

Our lives are finite not only in their span but in our capacity to do and act. That is the human condition. We yearn for
more in life than we can ever have. This is a fundamental fact
of existence captured in Augustine's famous formulation that
"our hearts are restless." This very restlessness is the fount
from which the development (or lack of development) of our
being takes shape. It explains why we are always on the way
and have not yet arrived. It explains why we never lose the
drive to know and the desire to love and be loved. It is a pilgrimage whose end has not yet come.

This open character of being human is something to be not only accepted but also celebrated. It means that life itself unfolds, in the etymological sense of the term, gradually—by steps. That fact should help us resist the idea that our lives, understood either in the spiritual or physical sense, need to move forward in lock step. We can always, despite difficulties, know and love more. The future that stands before us pulls us forward. To see that future as the infinite mystery which is God makes sense of the entire pilgrimage, is the essence of faith, and the sure ground of hope.

The anonymous fourteenth-century author of *The Cloud of Unknowing* wrote some other spiritual treatises among which was a little tract called the *Discernment of Stirrings*. In that treatise the *Cloud* author has some brief words on the elusive nature of God's presence who is found not in any pair of opposites like speaking/keeping silent or fasting/eating but "between them." He then goes on to say that in this life we do not fully know God through our efforts or our works. What we can, and should, do is affirm God in faith through simple love. He concludes:

> If God is your love and your purpose, the chief aim of your heart, it is all that you need in this life, although you never see more of him with the eye of reason your whole life long. Such a blind shot with the sharp dart of longing love will never miss its mark, which is God.

A Prayer

To you, O God, every heart stands open
and every will speaks;
no secret is hidden from you.
I implore you so to purify the intention of my heart
with the gift of your grace [or your Holy Ghost]
that I may love you perfectly and praise you
worthily. Amen.

This prayer stands at the head of *The Cloud of Unknowing*. It may have originated in Carthusian circles and may have been known as the prayer *ad postulandam gratiam Spiritus Sancti*—a prayer to "beg for the grace of the Holy spirit."

Like many collect prayers from the liturgy, it is succinct in stating both the actual condition of the person who prays and the grace which is desired. If we look carefully at it, the author states (implicitly, to be sure) the condition of the human heart as imperfect as well as the concomitant desire for the purification of such imperfection in order to love God better. The prayer, then, is a prayer that recognizes the need for conversion. The continual practice of conversion as turning from and turning toward underpins the *Cloud* author's whole notion of prayer, which he defines as "a devout reaching out directly to God in order to attain the good and to do away with evil" (*Cloud*, chap. 39). Note that that definition contains within it the aversion/conversion motif.

The *Cloud* author begins his treatise with the above prayer and, seventy-five chapters later, he ends his treatise with another prayer that complements the first:

> And I beseech almighty God that true peace, sane counsel and spiritual comfort in God with abundance of grace, always be with you and with all those who on earth love God. Amen.

These prayers are taken from the exemplary edition of *The Cloud of Unknowing*, edited with an introduction by James Walsh, S.J. (Mahwah, NJ: Paulist, 1981). The same editor has now produced a second volume from the *Cloud* author: *Pursuit of the Wisdom and Other Works by the Author of the Cloud of Unknowing* (Mahwah, NJ: Paulist, 1988).

A Note on Readings

Spiritual ascent literature is enormous. We list here only those works referred to in the text. The best edition of the Benedictine *Rule* is: *The Rule of Saint Benedict*, edited by Timothy Fry, O.S.B. (Collegeville, MN: The Liturgical Press, 1981). The basic spiritual writings of John Cassian, John Climacus, Gregory of Nyssa, Saint Bonaventure, Teresa of Avila, John of the Cross, etc., are all available in fresh translations in the Paulist series Classics of Western Spirituality. My information on Walter Hilton comes from Clifton Wolters's "The

English Mystics," in *The Study of Spirituality*, edited by Cheslyn Jones et al. (New York: Oxford University Press, 1986), pp. 328–37. It was in that essay that I found the quote from the *Cloud* author's *Discernment of Stirrings*. For Teresa of Avila's *Interior Castle* I used the edition of E. Allison Peers in the Image Book series (Garden City, NY: Doubleday, 1961). There is a succinct investigation of these issues in Thomas Merton's *Contemplative Prayer* (Garden City, NY: Doubleday Image, 1971); this book also appears under the title *The Climate of Monastic Prayer*. Evelyn Underhill's classic *Mysticism* (a reprint; New York: Dutton, 1961) is still extremely useful. A useful anthology in this area is *Understanding Mysticism*, edited by Richard Woods, O.P. (Garden City, NY: Doubleday, 1980).

On Jacques Maritain's mystical teachings, see Curtis L. Hancock, "Maritain on Mystical Contemplation," in *Understanding Maritain: Philosopher and Friend*, edited by Deal W. Hudson and Matthew J. Mancini (Macon, GA: Mercer University Press, 1987), pp. 257–70. That essay is a careful study of Jacques Maritain's *Degrees of Knowledge*, translated by Gerald Phelan (New York: Scribners, 1959). For an older scholastic treatment see Reginald Garrigou-Lagrange, *Christian Perfection and Contemplation* (Saint Louis, MO: Herder, 1937).

Søren Kierkegaard's stages may be found in *Either/Or* (Princeton: Princeton University Press, 1941) and *Fear and Trembling* (Princeton: Princeton University Press, 1941). In the latter work there is the discussion of Abraham as the Knight of Faith.

On anthropological stages, see Arnold von Gennep, *Rites of Passage* (Chicago: University of Chicago Press, 1961). Baron von Hugel's discussion of the analogies of growth and the spiritual life are in volume one of *The Mystical Element of Religion*, 2 vols. (London: Dent, 1909), pp. 50ff.

A work that has informed this chapter is Mary Durkin and Andrew Greeley, *A Church to Come Home to* (Chicago: St. Thomas More, 1982). I have used this material in *Faith Rediscovered: Coming Home to Catholicism* (Mahwah, NJ: Paulist, 1987).

Walter Conn's *Christian Conversion* (Mahwah, NJ: Paulist, 1986) can be supplemented by the same author's article "Conversion," in *The Westminster Dictionary of Christian Spirituality*, edited by Gordon S. Wakefield (Philadelphia: Westminster, 1983).

James Fowler's *Stages of Faith* (San Francisco, CA: Harper and Row, 1981) was the subject of an interesting review symposium in *Horizons* 9 (1982), pp. 104–26 which includes a concluding response by the author.

Lawrence S. Cunningham, *The Catholic Heritage* (New York: Crossroad, 1983) has a chapter on pilgrimage with an appended bibliography of sources.

APPENDIX

TEACHING ABOUT PRAYER

At the end of his now famous handbook *Foundations of Christian Faith* (ET: 1978), Karl Rahner has an appendix in which he argues for the legitimacy of composing short creedal statements while providing some examples of such creeds that he himself has composed. By analogy, we could say that there is a legitimacy in being not only consumers of prayers but creators of them, just as Rahner urges us to be creators of creeds.

This is hardly a new exercise. It is clear that the greatest of our theologians have not only regularly written prayers but have also been among the preeminent composers of hymns, as the memory of Thomas Aquinas, Martin Luther, and John Henry Newman makes clear. Similarly, the greatest of spiritual doctors are also ranked as great theologians when their books have been oriented not to the theologians but to those who wish to pray. Thus, the two women who have been named doctors of the church—Saint Catherine of Siena and Saint Teresa of Avila—were not professional theologians, but both wrote books to which theologians turn for nourishment. In the pages of this book we have considered these people frequently to see how their prayers can aid us in seeking understanding in the life of faith. It is well to remember that one of the greatest of Christian classics—*The Confessions* of Saint

Augustine—can be read as an extended prayer of both praise and repentance. In fact, as Peter Brown has argued in his authoritative biography of the saint, Augustine found the prayer form a very persuasive vehicle for doing the kind of speculative theology he wanted to do in *The Confessions*.

It is thus clear that the prayers which have come down to us through tradition are a valid source of theological reflection. We have already noted that there is an uninterrupted tradition of commentary on the Lord's Prayer which begins in the second century and continues to the present day. Each age finds its own way of seeing and responding to the prayer that Aquinas calls the perfect prayer of the Christian. It is my fond hope to put together an anthology of these commentaries because they shed much light on the depths of both private and liturgical prayer, since the commentary tradition reflects both the individual and communal response to that prayer.

How, in the concrete, can we enter that long dialogue with the tradition of prayer in the church? This book, as a whole, was an attempt to say a first word about such a dialogue, but there are also more concrete and specific ways in which we might encounter the tradition of prayer. Let me offer a few suggestions.

First, we might try to offset the familiarity of our formula prayers by attempting to recast them in our own words. This can be done as a way of getting away from the half-remembered resonances that such prayers bring with them. What, for example, would the *Ave Maria* look like if we were to rewrite it in words that express our own Marian devotion or our own understanding of the Virgin in our spiritual life? This prayer, for example, would look a good deal different if we were to think of Mary more as a model and less as an intercessor and vice versa.

Recasting prayers also helps to show that the exercise of paraphrase rarely does justice to the original. Would anyone, for example, prefer Dante's scholastic paraphrase in the *Purgatorio* to the original of the Lord's Prayer? The linguistic intractability of original "classic" prayers illustrates not only their value but also presents the "problem" of their receptivity in various cultural ages.

Secondly, we might simply compose prayer formulas for ordinary use. Most of us do not struggle for our sustenance in any dramatic fashion (that fact is worth pondering in its own right); so it is hard for us to think of our food as "gifts" as the standard grace before meals names it. Most families receive their meals as naturally as they breathe air and walk forward. How, in our privileged circumstances, do we recapture that primordial sense of gratitude which is at the heart of all real prayer? How, in short, do we "translate" the words of a prayer so that they reflect not our capacity to remember but our capacity to experience? In the exercise of "translation" we need to move beyond the mere surface of paraphrase if this exercise is to bear good fruit.

It is increasingly common for people to create ritual words for their own use like "personalized" wedding vows. It would be a most useful (and spiritual) activity for people to compose an entire vade mecum of prayers for all of the celebrations of family and community. The common objection that such prayers are often sentimental and banal (and they are often sentimental and banal) should not deter us. The *Raccolta* (an anthology of indulgenced prayers in the Catholic church) is filled with banal prayers. Use and longevity sort out the worst of our sentiments. The very practice of composing prayers offers a further antidote to overly poetic effusions. Such exercises provide us with the further advantage of seeing quite precisely how language falters in the very act of giving expression to those truths which we desire to enunciate from a deep personal conviction as opposed to an academic exercise of explication. The exercise of composition, in short, is an exercise in the limited use of language to express deep belief as opposed to banal sentiments.

Thirdly, there is the issue of belief(s). Few of us, I suspect, have followed Rahner's urging to compose creeds of our own. If we were asked to set out what, at base, we truly believed, one wonders how closely our creed would track the words (or even the sentiments) of the Apostles' Creed. It is easy enough to say "I believe in the Resurrection of the Dead" but it should take us up short if one were to inquire: "What do you really mean when you say that?" By converting our creedal affirmations into prayerful statements, we might come closer to answering that second question which we find so easy to evade or ignore under normal circumstances.

This kind of exercise is simply a variation on the old practice of responding to a text (a "scene") of scripture in a prayerful way: It is a step from what is before us so that we can internalize it in a vividly concrete and prayerful fashion. In fact, the composition of prayers in response to our reading of the scriptures is a variation on monastic *lectio* which, as we have noted throughout this work, should ultimately lead to *oratio* and, ideally, to *contemplatio*.

Creeds serve both doctrinal and catechetical functions, but it must be remembered they also serve doxological ones: They are statements of faith and praise. It is not simply accidental that we recite the creed as a coda to the liturgy of the Word. Our statement "I believe" or "We believe" at the end of the homily has a worship function to it: It is an affirmation that we are in the company of those who accept the proclaimed Word and, in that affirmation, we are pray-ers as well as believers. Creeds are also ecclesial proclamations so that, when recast, they should not only be *my* creed but, in some sense *our* creed.

This is not a trivial point. Can we set out what we believe (a creed) and can we transform that statement into a prayer? If we are committed, say, to Jesus then we can say "I have faith in Jesus" and "I believe in you, Jesus." The first is a formulation of belief; the second is a prayer, but the focus of both affirmations is the same.

Other doctrinal formulations are a bit harder to convert into prayer. I have seen, in a very conservative religious newspaper, an advertisement of an obscure religious order that describes itself as devoted to the Immaculate Mother of God and the Magisterium (a curious creed in its own right!). About Mary, it would be easy to pray and/or compose prayers, but what would a prayer that focuses in on the Magisterium look like? The rule of thumb runs something like this: If we accept the Second Vatican Council's notion that there is a hierarchy of truths then the closer one is to the basic truths, the simpler it is to pray and/or convert doctrines into prayer. It is a lot easier, for example, to turn the mystery of the Trinity into a prayer than it is to pray about birth control except, in the latter example, a prayer of desperation: "Please, Lord, let me be (or not be) pregnant."

Prayer is also a plea for belief at those times when we feel belief slipping away. Prayer can articulate our doubts as well as the assurances of our belief. It is well to remember that the Book of Psalms—which is *the* prayer book of biblical religion—records both unshakeable faith and the cry that comes *de profundis.* Our prayers that attempt to pray for belief rather than those which come from belief bring us very close to the foundations of who we are as religious persons. As Walter Brueggemann has noted in his splendid *The Message of the Psalms* (1984) there are Psalms of orientation that stand in tension with Psalms of disorientation in the Psalter; but beyond those are the Psalms that point forward to a new orientation which, in Brueggemann's words, "speak boldly about a new gift from God, a fresh intrusion that makes all things new."

The obvious deduction from the above is that one can get a clearer and deeper notion of one's own personal credo by the simple expedient of attempting to turn one's beliefs into prayer. What does not convert to prayer is probably epiphenomenal in one's life or becomes a kind of subordinate clause in a prayer that directs itself to far more basic truths. Prayers of this kind can be cast in the form of extended meditations on basic Christian beliefs. When prayers of this kind are done in the hand of a master we also receive theology at a high level in the bargain. A model of this kind of enterprise is Karl Rahner's *Prayers for a Lifetime* (New York: Crossroad, 1984), which is a collection of prayers composed over the public career of the eminent theologian and presented to him on the occasion of his eightieth birthday.

The fourth strategy is a mirror image of the third. We can go to the prayers that form part of our inheritance and try to determine what truths they carry by simply asking: Stripped of "prayer rhetoric," what is being said here? What basic Christian truths stand at the base of, say, our eucharistic canons? When one takes a close look at prayers like that it is surprising what one sees. Prayers, even when paraphrased, tend to be far more linguistically nourishing than the technical language of conciliar statements and/or theological precisions. For that reason alone theologians and other scholars in the sacred sciences need to pay attention to prayer as a theological datum.

Finally, it is a good exercise to try to use the events, instruments, occasions, and people of our everyday existence as subjects for prayer. Michael Quoist was a master at this strategy in his ability to rework everything from a piece of currency to a playing of the radio into a prayer. Examples may be found in his book *Prayers of a Life* (1965).

The danger of this strategy is the temptation to become "poetic" in the most maudlin and banal fashion or to become socially or politically "hip" to the current headlines. Anyone who does not think this is so might try—if they have the energy for it—to reread a 1960s "relevant" prayerbook like Malcolm Boyd's *Are You Running With Me, Jesus?*

The merit of the strategy is to remove prayer from the arena of "Thee, Thou, Vouchsafe, etc." into the less-than-exalted world of the way we live each day. Prayers that center on our families, fears, jobs, hopes, and failures as well as our possessions and our pleasures bring prayer (as long as we do not turn these exercises into simply personal ruminations) into the arena of the immediate. Prayer demands a certain purity of language, which is why we have noted its affinity with the poetic process understood as care for language and not necessarily an exalted use of language. Furthermore, prayer rooted in the ordinary experiences of life has a long warrant in the Christian tradition, receiving a full treatment in Carmelite writers like Brother Lawrence and Saint Thérèse of Lisieux who tried to keep the life of prayer very close to the ordinary life of what they considered to be their own ordinary lives.

This same strategy is useful by doing what is at least as old as *The Spiritual Exercises* of Saint Ignatius Loyola. Ignatian praxis recommends moving from a meditative consideration of the Gospel to a prayer based on that consideration. One can personalize the Gospels, as the church has done *ab initio*, by turning to the Gospels in prayer. That strategy provides not only Bible study but devotion.

Here, a notebook is useful. It might contain fragments which can be short prayers in themselves as well as a place where our prayers in response to reading can be saved.

As a "classroom" exercise it might be well to think of how prayers might look if they were demanded of us for a specific occasion. What would a prayer for universal peace look like if we were asked to recite one with a group representing different religious traditions? How would we articulate our faith in the gracefulness of the world when we are asked to pray to comfort people who have just suffered a terrible tragedy? What would prayers look like that would articulate our hopes/fears for our future, the future of our family, nation, and world?

Andrew Greeley has recently suggested using a video camera to record parent's feelings for their children's future when, as infants, they are brought for baptism. Greeley's suggestion is meant to help the parents (and the children) to have a video record of the hope that springs from the beginning of life. It is a splendid suggestion which could be fleshed out by suggesting that parents might compose prayer books in which significant moments of a child's growth might be commemorated and then passed on to the young person when he or she reaches his or her majority.

From its beginnings, the church has encouraged prayer at morning and evening. Done officially as lauds and vespers, this practice forms the basis of the daily office of the church's liturgy. There is a plethora of abbreviated offices based on this custom. It would be an instructive exercise for people to create their own office book. A prayer notebook might be used simply for people to note Psalms that they most love and respond to and to divide them into Psalms for the morning and evening. One need not use the entire Psalter; a selection of Psalms could form the core of a daily book of prayers to be used morning and evening.

One source that is particularly useful for the recasting and formulation of prayers and liturgies is the Women-Church movement which, among other things, has paid particular attention to those issues which seem to me crucial when thinking about prayer: the character of language, the intentionality that drives language, the relationship of prayer to theological postures. I would be less than frank if I did not say that some of what the Women-Church movement stands for strikes me as sectarian and elitist but, having said that, it is equally true that those who participate in the movement have produced very interesting prayer models and the theory that justifies such experiments. The best source for both theory and examples of liturgies is Rosemary Radford Ruether, *Women-Church: Theology and Practice* (San Francisco: Harper and Row, 1985), which provides some extremely creative ideas about prayer and liturgy. What has fascinated me most about the literature from this movement is the deep struggle with the problem of language (and not merely at the level of scrubbing out "sexist" construction) as a vehicle for the articulation of belief.

Finally, while I have warned about becoming too "poetic" about prayer, the tradition of poetry in English is a fine source for understanding the nature of prayer. Not only has this tradition a number of poems which are, in fact, prayers but the prayerful impulse is quite often found in poems that, on the face of it, do not seem to be *ex professo* religious. That point has been abundantly made by any number of fine scholars (William Noon, Louis Martz, Justus George Lawler, Nathan Scott, etc.) and it is a conviction that I share. It is for this reason that I have not hesitated to appeal to the poetic tradition in this work with the hope that such usage might well incite others to do the same. The bibliography at the end of chapter 2 provides an entry into the important field of poetics and spirituality.

INDEX

Accedia, 58
Alonso-Schokel, Luis, 74
Altars of worship and reservation
  separation of, 62
Ambrose, 70
Anselm of Canterbury, 4
Anthony, 59
Anthony of the Desert, 93, 140
Are You Running With Me,
  Jesus? (Boyd), 198
Aristotle, 2
Ascesis
  reconceptualization of, 58
Asceticism
  purpose of, 58
Athanasius, 140
Auerbach, Eric, 83
Auerbach, Erich, 8
Augustine, 20, 45, 93, 140, 188

Base Christian communities, 79
Benedict, 172
Benediction of Blessed Sacrament, 124
Bible. *See* Scriptures
Blessed Sacrament
  devotion to, 125
Bloy, Leon, 28

Body language, 54
Boff, Leonardo, 43
Bonaventure, 33, 172
Book of Common Prayer, 148
Boyd, Malcolm, 198
Bradshaw, Paul, 55
Bremond, Henri, 30
Brown, Peter, 134, 142, 194
Brueggemann, Walter, 197
Buber, Martin, 12, 14, 31, 32–33
Buhlmann, Walbert, 154

Can We Still Call God "Father"?
  (Mangan), 163
Canon Law, Code of, 124
Canonical criticism, 81
Carolingian Renaissance, 107
Cassian, John, 43, 168, 172
Catherine of Siena, 193
Catholic Experience, The
  (Cunningham), 78
Catholic Heritage, The
  (Cunningham), 185
Centering prayer, 38
Charlesworth, James H., 67
Chesterton, G.K., 143
Childs, Brevard, 82
Christian Approach to the Bible,
  The (Dom Charlier), 73

Christian Conversion: A Developmental Interpretation of Autonomy and Surrender (Conn), 181
Christian living, 64
Church
  as countersign, 160–161
  as diverse community, 160–161
  as learner and teacher, 165
  and local worshipping community, 155
  relationship to human culture, 164
  as servant, 160
  and social justice, 162
Church of the Future, The (Buhlmann), 154
Climacus, John, 172, 183
Cloud of Unknowing, 138, 173, 189
Columba of Iona, 46
Coming of the World Church, The (Buhlmann), 154
Confessions of St. Augustine, 20–21, 140, 193–194
Conjectures of a Guilty Bystander (Merton), 167
Conn, Walter, 181–182, 184
Conversion, 180
  as prayer, 182
Corpus Christi, feast of, 124
Council of Chalcedon, 95
Cousins, Ewert, 85, 98
Creeds
  doctrinal, catechetical and doxological functions of, 196
  personal, 195

Crosby, David, 43
Cult and Controversy: The Worship of the Eucharist Outside of Mass (Mitchell), 113

Dalrymple, John, 139
Dante Alighieri, 173
Das Gebet (Heiler), 11
Day, Dorothy, 147
de Chardin, Teilhard, 85, 169, 170
de Foucauld, Charles, 114
de Voragine, Jacopus, 140
Degrees of Knowledge, The (Maritain), 173
Devotionalism
  decline of, 56
Discernment of Stirrings, 189
Discipline
  reconceptualization of, 58
Divine Comedy (Dante), 173
Dulles, Avery, 160
Dunne, John, 166

Eckhart, Meister, 14, 32, 58
Eliade, Mircea, 7, 12, 17
  and ritualized gestures, 62
Eliot, T.S., 29
Eucharist
  apex of Christ's presence, 119
  communal nature of, 116
  as great mystery of faith, 117
  and needs of destitute, 120
  real presence and union with Christ, 62
  reservation of, 117–118
  sacrament of ecclesiality, 123
  See also Blessed Sacrament
Eucharistic theology, 62

Eucharistic Worship, Instruction on, 119, 127
Evagrius of Pontus, 35
Evangelization in the Modern World (Paul VI), 161–162

Faith
  acts of juxtaposed to prayer, 21
  and other religious traditions, 166
  and prayer, 24
Faith Rediscovered (Cunningham), 181
Fiorenza, Francis Schussler, 161
Fire and Light: The Saints and Theology (Thompson), 138
First Communion
  as a rite of passage, 112
First Urban Christians: The Social World of the Apostle Paul, The (Meeks), 100
Foundational Theology (Fiorenza), 161
Foundations of Christian Faith (Rahner), 122, 193
Fowler, James, 174
Francis of Assisi, 22, 32, 85, 93, 132, 140, 143, 167
  prayer of, 44
Francis Xavier, 93
Freud, Sigmund, 184
Frye, Northrup, 83
Fuchs, Joseph, 18
Fundamental option, 18–19
Fundamentalist temptation, 80
The Future of Illusion (Freud), 184

Gestures, 49–68
God's Encounter with Man: A Contemporary Approach to Prayer (Nedoncelle), 99
Golden Legend, The (de Voragine), 140
Golden String, The (Griffiths), 165
Good Apprentice, The (Murdoch), 39
Gratitude
  in prayer, 195
Greeley, Andrew, 181, 199
Gregory the Great, 69
Gregory of Nyssa, 138, 173
Griffiths, Bede, 165
Guardini, Romano, 24
Guigo the Carthusian, 49

Hammarskjold, Dag, 14–17, 19
Harmony
  in what we say and do, 156
Heaney, Seamus, 172
Heart of the Matter, The (de Chardin), 170
Heiler, Friedrich, 11, 18
Herbert, George, 16
Hierophany, 17
Hilton, Walter, 172, 186
Humility
  and prayer, 166

I and Thou (Buber), 31
Idea of the Holy, The (Otto), 12
Ignatius Loyola, 140, 198
Imitation of Christ, The, 14
Immanence and transcendence, 51
Independence
  economic and the larger community, 153

Isaac of Nineveh, Saint, 151
Itinerarium (Bonaventure), 172

James, William, 10
Jesus Christ
  emphasis on divinity of, 95
  examples of authentic prayer,
    106
  human and cosmic, 143
  as *mysterium*, 62
  and our relationship with God,
    20
  as pray-er, 91
  prayer as a Jew, 106
  radical of gospels, 143
  social manifestations of Jesus'
    prayer life, 105
  surplus of meaning in, 103
  as teacher of prayer, 106
  transcendent and immanent,
    62
  unique prayer of, 93
  view of influences our prayer,
    143
  as visible sign of God's pres-
    ence, 97
Jesus Through the Centuries
  (Pelikan), 84
John of the Cross, 14, 32, 138,
  140, 173, 184
John Damascene, 98
John Paul II
  and personalism, 162
Johnston, William, 155
Joyce, James, 30, 152
Julian, 184
Justin, 154

Kasper, Walter, 94–95
Katz, Steven, 131–132
Keating, Thomas, 57

Kierkegaard, Soren, 175–176
Kneeling
  at Mass, 60–61
Knox, Ronald, 60
Korczak, Janusz, 158

Ladder of Divine Love, The
  (Climacus), 172
Ladder of Perfection, The
  (Hilton), 172
Language
  changed by authentic sense of
    God, 32
  religious, 34
Larranaga, Ignacio, 139
Lawler, Justus George, 200
Lawrence, Brother, 198
Lectio divina, 74, 75–76
Lectio-meditatio-oratio, 74–77
Leech, Kenneth, 119
Lex orandi, lex credendi, 5
Liberation
  gospel and, 162
Liberation theology, 43, 79, 143,
  145, 164
Liturgy
  celebrates differentness, 64
  centrality of, 116
  multicultural, 63
  new, 59
  and privitization of faith, 122
  public worship, 59
  and sacramental and incarna-
    tional realities, 122
  social bond of, 100
  vertical and horizontal dimen-
    sions of, 99
Lord's prayer, 36
  as a classic, 37
  standing for, 61

Louth, Andrew, 87
Love of Learning and the Desire for God, The (Dom Leclercq), 74
Luther, Martin, 193

MacGinty, Gerard, 75
Mackey, James, 94
Mangan, Celine, 163
Maritain, Jacques, 30, 173
Markings (Hammarskjold), 15–16
Martz, Louis, 30, 200
Mary, 133
  attributes of, 145
  and context of Christology, 103
  as model of our prayer, 146
  as model and source of doctrine, 143–144
  as new Eve, 144
  as sign of our hope of union with Christ, 144
  as Theotokos, 144
Mass
  significance of attendance at, 60
Mass on the World, The (de Chardin), 169
Maurin, Peter, 159
Maximus the Confessor, 36
Meeks, Wayne, 100
Merton, Thomas, 33, 57, 97–98, 114, 132, 141, 161, 165, 167, 182
  prayer of, 101–102
Message of the Psalms, The (Brueggemann), 197
Metanoia, 177–178
Miles, Margaret, 58

Mind's Journey, The, 33
Mitchell, Nathan, 113, 125–126
Models
  different from celebrities, 146
Models of prayer, 131–150
Muggaridge, Anne Roche, 115
Murdoch, Iris, 39
Mystical Element in Religion, The (von Hugel), 174

Nedoncelle, Maurice, 99
New Book of Christian Prayers, The (Castle), 87
Newman, John Henry, 193
Night (Wiesel), 35
Nine Ways of Prayer of Saint Dominic, The, 55–56
Noon, William, 200

Odes of Solomon, The (Charlesworth), 67, 90
Origen, 37, 55, 87
Otto, Rudolph, 12

Pascal, Blaise, 13–14
Passion narratives, 83
Pattern prayers, 18
Peace
  kiss of, 61
  sign of, 61
Pelikan, Jaroslav, 84
Percy, Walker, 72
Perrin, Father, 16
Pilgrimage 185–186
Plotinus, 173, 177
Poemen, Abba, 142, 148
Polis, 151, 156
Portrait of the Artist as a Young Man, A (Joyce), 30, 152
Prayer (Von Balthasar), 121

Prayer
  and accompanying gestures, 50
  authenticity of, 105–106
  basic energizers of, 44
  bodily discomfort and, 57
  centering, 38
  centrality of, 141
  as characteristic of all religion, 11
  with Christ, 99
  condition of, 22
  definition of, 9
  demystification of, 104
  desolation in, 138–139
  Eucharistic, 120
  and faith, 9
  formulaic, meaning of, 41
  and fundamental relationship, 9
  link with larger community, 151–171
  models of, 131–150
  moving from local to universal, 152, 168
  new uses of words in, 45
  as plea for belief, 197
  political character of, 151–171
  recitation of as essence, 157
  redefined, 58
  reflective component of, 43
  as relationship, 17–18, 28
  as relationship of whole person to God, 58
  separates philosophy from religion, 11
  as social phenomenon, 59
  specificity of, 158
  subjects for, 198
  ways it becomes speech, 29

Prayers from Theology (Rahner), 24
Prayers of a Life (Quoist), 198
Prayers for a Lifetime (Rahner), 197
Primary speech, 31

Quietism, 97
Quoist, Michael, 198

Raccolta, The, 195
Rahner, Karl, 22, 24, 29, 30, 45, 90, 122–123, 140, 154, 163, 197
Real presence
  shift away from, 114
Religion
  conservativeness of, 33
Ricoeur, Paul, 39
Rituals, personal, 195
Rubrics, 55
Ruusbroec, John, 91
Ruether, Rosemary Radford, 200

Sabatier, Auguste, 11
Sacra pagina, 4
Sacred, intrusion of, 8
Sacred language, 31
Saints
  as fellow pray-ers, 142
  and the imitation of Christ, 143
  as models of Christian living, 143
  models for our prayer, 138, 141
  unreality of tradition, 147
Sapiential reading, 73
Scott, Nathan, 200
Scriptures
  boredom and, 72

christological reading of, 81
and culture, 79–80
and liturgy, 74
and prayer, 69
and prayer life, 70
Sensing Your Hidden Presence (Larranaga), 139
Silence, 57
Simon Stylites, Saint, 141
Simple Prayer (Dalrymple), 139
Sin
   aversion to, 178
   definition of, 180
Social self, 168
Soul-friend, 148
Spiritual elites, 65
Spiritual Espousals, The (Ruusbroec), 91
Spiritual Exercises, The (Ignatius Loyola), 198
Spiritual growth
   by stages, 173, 175
Spiritual life
   increased appetite for, 56
Spirituality, contemporary
   appeal of, 65
Stages of Faith: The Psychology of Human Development and Quest for Meaning (Fowler), 174
Subsidiarity, 158
Systematic Theology (Tillich), 23

Teresa, Mother, 133, 134, 167
Teresa of Avila, 32, 173, 193
Tertullian, 37, 55
Theophanies, 12
Therese of Lisieux, 138, 198
Thibon, Gustave, 16

Thomas Aquinas, 20, 37, 45, 56, 187, 193, 194
Thompson, William H., 138
Tillich, Paul, 22–23
Tracy, David, 37, 85, 138
Transcendence and immanence, 61
Treasury of Irish Religious Verse (Murray), 47

Ulanov, Ann, 31
Ulanov, Barry, 31

van Gennep, Arnold, 174
Varieties of Religious Experience, The (James), 10
Vatican Council II
   and Christian humanism, 160
   and ecumenism and non-Christian religions, 155
   and Eucharist as center of community, 115
   eucharistic theology of, 62
   and Eucharistic presence, 111
   hierarchy of truths in Catholicism, 103
   hierarchy of truths, 196
   and liturgy, 74, 127
   prayer and scriptures, 70
   reforms of, 126
   and rejection of other religious traditions, 102
   and world church, 154, 163
Vincent de Paul, 133
Von Balthasar, Hans Urs, 121

Waddell, Helen, 107
Ware, Timothy, 98
Watkin, E.I., 30

Weil, Simone, 16, 17, 111
Wiesel, Elie, 35
Women-Church movement,
    199–200
*Women-Church: Theology and
    Practice* (Ruether), 200

World Council of Churches
    and Eucharist, 116
Worship
    feminist, 60

Zappa, Frank, 131